# THE REAL JESUS
# SEEN IN
# BLACK AND WHITE
# FROM
# THE RESURRECTED SPIRIT
# OF DIXON FRYE

## BY
## J. WAYNE FRYE

All royalties from the sales of this book will be donated to charitable organizations.

## The Real Jesus Seen in Black and White
## From the Resurrected Spirit of Dixon Frye

**TO: My long gone grandfather, Worth Buren "Dixon" Frye, who never let religion keep him from being compassionate and tolerant. Though I did not realize it at the time, sitting by his side in the porch swing and listening to him pontificate on life was a valuable educational exercise and a lesson in how to never let others do your thinking for you. I never realized the esteem in which I held him until it was too late to utter these simple words, "Granddaddy, you are a wise and kind man who taught me the value of understanding that those who sit in judgment of others have no idea of what being a Christian really is."**

**And as always, to my muse, Lynton Globa Viñas**

Catalogue Number: 2015-2453577

ISBN: 978-1-928183-20-4

**Fireside Books – Victoria, British Columbia**
Part of the Peninsula Publishing Consortium

J. Wayne Frye

The Real Jesus Seen in Black and White
From the Resurrected Spirit of Dixon Frye

TABLE OF CONTENTS

J. Wayne Frye

# The Real Jesus Seen in Black and White
# From the Resurrected Spirit of Dixon Frye

## About the Author

Wayne Frye's *Aaron Adams, Girl* series books and *Lynton* adventures are popular with mystery readers. He provides satirical political commentary to many Canadian newspapers, and his books on politics have created a great deal of controversy.

He has written marketing/advertising textbooks, been a highly successful U.S. university hockey coach, professor, university president and served as a marketing consultant to hockey teams and motion picture companies. He has been cited for his work with inner-city gangs in Los Angeles and been active in the anti-globalization movement. He became a Canadian citizen in 2003 and lives in Ladysmith, British Columbia and Laguna, Philippines.

### Some Other Books by J. Wayne Frye

*Hockey Mania and the Mystery of Nancy Running Elk*
*Something Evil in the Darkness at Hopkins House*
*How Hockey Saved a Jew From the Holocaust:*
*The Rudi Ball Story*
*The Catastrophic Calamities of a Village Idiot*
*Fighting for Justice in the Land of Hypocrisy*
*The Girl Who Stirred up the Whirlwind*
*The Girl Who Motivated Murder Most Foul*
*The Girl Who Said Goodbye for the Last Time*
*Fall From Apocalypse*
*Armageddon Now*
*Worth*
*When Jesus Came to Jersey as the Son of Thunder*
*When Jesus Came to Canada to Lead an Indigenous Rebellion*
*Canadian Angels of Mercy – Nurses in Times of Peril*
*Points of Rebellion: Aboriginals Who Fought for Justice*
*Lynton Walks on Water*
*Lynton Curls Her Hair*
*Lynton and the Vampire at Taygaytay Manor*
*Lynton Buys a Cell-Phone and Hears the Voice of Doom*
*Lynton and the Ghosts at the Mansion on Balete Drive*
*Chablis: Avenging Angel for the Forgotten*
*In the City of Lost Hope*
*Chablis and the Terrorist*
*Pursuit*
*The Disappearance*
*Chablis and the Dildo from Hell*

J. Wayne Frye

**The Real Jesus Seen in Black and White**
**From the Resurrected Spirit of Dixon Frye**

## PROLOGUE
## SUNDAY SCHOOL LESSON FROM
## THE REVEREND DIXON FRYE

I was watching the traffic whiz by. It was one of my favourite past times as a child when visiting my grandparents on the weekends. In fact, each day of the week I counted off the time until Friday night when I would be carted off for the weekend to a place that was so often a refuge from a turbulent childhood where, in my home, drinking and partying were the norm, though physical violence was a rarity. The safe haven of my grandparents was a respite from the turbulence of a home where my alcoholic father would often make life untenable for my mother and me.

My grandmother sat in a rocker knitting. My grandfather and I were in the swing. It swayed rhythmically as I looked up at him and said, "Most people are in church on Sunday's granddaddy. How come we aren't there this morning?"

## The Real Jesus Seen in Black and White
## From the Resurrected Spirit of Dixon Frye

My grandmother, a coy smile curling her lips, said, "Go ahead Dixon, tell him why the Frye's are a rarely seen sight in church."

My grandfather was a man of few words, but those words were coated with wisdom. As time has passed, I often reflect on his words and realize, though he only had a third grade education, he had the wisdom of Socrates. He said "I'll do that Vada. The boy is old enough to know that church is full of people who frankly, if they gonna be in heaven, I'd rather be in hell than spend eternity with a bunch of hypocrites like the ones I see parading into church on Sunday's while they do the devil's work the rest of the week."

My grandmother, also an uneducated person with great depth of wisdom, interjected, "Yep, tell the boy all about your ideas on religion, Dixon."

Now, at this time I was maybe 7 or 8 years old, so each day was an adventure in learning. That morning I was about to learn a valuable lesson from a grandfather who was probably one of the most respected men in North Carolina. How that respect had come about is itself a lesson in religion – the religion that does not come from a Bible, but from the heart. My grandfather had endured the Great Depression, and like so many who had survived that abomination, his life and outlook were tempered by a time when the U.S. government proved to be callous and uncaring. He

# The Real Jesus Seen in Black and White
# From the Resurrected Spirit of Dixon Frye

had been a lifeline to many wanders who travelled the roads of America in the 1920's and 1930's looking for work in a nation that had basically, because of the boom and bust cycle of capitalism, been thrown into a morass of economic misery that was much worse than the collapse caused by the malfeasance of George W. Bush from 2001 to 2009. Though Bush's ignorance and service to the moneyed class at the expense of sane governance was tempered right away by the dedication and steady stewardship of America's first black president, Barrack Obama, there was no such hope in 1920, as the ignorance of the American people led to a steady stream of three Republican Presidents who muttered asinine comments like Calvin Coolidge, who brilliantly offered his assessment of the situation by saying, "Unemployment occurs when people are out of work." With brilliant observations like that to fight the coming calamity, one can see why they called him "Silent Cal," because he served the nation and himself best when he kept quiet. His predecessor, Warren Harding, another Republican with dubious rhetorical skills once said that poor people were simply part of God's grand plan for humanity. I am sure that was comforting to those who went to bed hungry at night, knowing that their poverty was simply part of a grand and glorious plan by the great deity that had anointed the USA as his sovereign representative on earth to carry out his will, which, of course, included making sure that capitalism flourished.

## The Real Jesus Seen in Black and White
## From the Resurrected Spirit of Dixon Frye

Then of course, these two buffoons as my granddad liked to call them, were followed by a man who simply sat by and did nothing when the whole house of cards built by the moneyed class collapsed into a pile of useless stocks, bonds and deflated money. Herbert Hoover was, himself, part of the moneyed class, but his wealth was protected by a smart father. Like most people born with a silver spoon in their mouths, he felt that the poor were there to serve the wealthy and privileged, and those at the top had no responsibility to the vast, unwashed masses. He, like Silent Cal, should have kept his mouth shut. He attributed the collapse and the depression to the poor expecting too much from government. He said, "Economic depression cannot be cured by legislative action or executive pronouncement. Economic wounds must be healed by the action of the cells of the economic body, the producers and consumers themselves. Just wait and the marketplace will make the proper adjustments." That kind of lunacy is what the Hollywood Crown Prince of Buffoonery, Ronald Reagan, was pronouncing in the 1980's – "let the market work its magic." Of course, my grandfather always said that the idiots making those kinds of pronouncements like Harding, Coolidge and Hoover did, all had a good paying job courtesy of the American taxpayer, while the rest of the country had to worry about where their next meal was coming from. Then he would always add, "And them Presidents got a chef paid by the taxpayers fixing their meals."

## The Real Jesus Seen in Black and White
## From the Resurrected Spirit of Dixon Frye

Dixon had run a general store in Farmer, North Carolina and managed to build a good business supplying the bootleggers with the sugar they needed to formulate the euphoric elixir that helped people forget the grinding poverty that the Republicans in government saw, as they do today, to be the fault of those who were poor. It is easy to blame the poor for being poor, but takes real courage to tackle the root of the problem which is an unforgiving system of greed called capitalism that has no heart and no compassion. The Republicans running the government from 1921 until 1933, were as they are today, heartless servants of the moneyed class who believed that the natural order of things was to allow those at the top of the economic ladder to rule with impunity over those less fortunate victims of greed. This is the world as my grandfather saw it, and it was a world that I came to comprehend at an early age. Though our family was better off economically than most, I was always able to see that this system was probably one of the worst forms of economic enslavement ever conceived by the privileged class. As I grew and matured, I often reflected on my grandfather's wise assessment of economics. He could in a precise, down-to-earth kind of way thoroughly articulate the maladies of a system that always worked from the top down so that those at the bottom were only left with table scraps to fight over while those at the top laughed all the way to the bank in their chauffeured limousines.

## The Real Jesus Seen in Black and White
## From the Resurrected Spirit of Dixon Frye

My grandfather saw religion, not as a servant of the poor, but as a safety valve for the rich to use so they could convince the poor that their reward would be in heaven, and they would, therefore, accept their lot on earth willingly, because in the afterlife, they would walk streets paved with gold in that grand palace in the sky. One of his most profound musings was when he would say to me, "Boy, when a man tells you he is a Christian, put your hand on your billfold."

That Sunday, as the swing moved gracefully back and forth and the unceasing roar of the traffic on the busy highway in front of the house caused an occasional vibration when a large 18 wheeler would roll by, my grandfather said something that still rings in my ears today. "Boy, them there Christians ain't got no monopoly on goodness. In fact, they some of the gosh-darn evilest people I know. Pointing your fingers at people and praising yourself ain't Jesus-like at all. I ain't saying there never was no Jesus, but if 'un they was, believe me, the man I read about would have the door slammed in his face if he showed up at most churches. They wouldn't let a shabby-dressed, long-haired, sandal-shoed, dark-skinned, probably un-bathed rebel walk into their place of worship. You can bet your bottom dollar on that."

My wise grandmother laughed and said, "And that Wayne is your Sunday school lesson from the Reverend Dixon Frye."

J. Wayne Frye

**The Real Jesus Seen in Black and White
From the Resurrected Spirit of Dixon Frye**

## CHAPTER 1
## MINIONS OF DESPAIR

My grandfather was renowned for his generosity to people who were down on their luck. During the depression, he shared as much food as he could with the wanderers that came by his general store, but he had a hard time feeding his own family, so he could only do so much, but he did what he could to lighten their load. There was a church nearby that, as is the case today, had empty pews but never opened its doors to offer homeless travellers in search of work a pew for the night. However, Dixon Frye built a lean-to behind his store so that travellers would have a roof over their heads and some freshly turned straw to rest on for the night. He pointed out to me often that it seemed the preachers got through the depression just fine as their congregations kept tossing a few pennies into the collection plate, no doubt out of hope the Lord would somehow maybe give them a little good luck that was in such short supply.

## The Real Jesus Seen in Black and White
## From the Resurrected Spirit of Dixon Frye

He would often laugh and say, "The collection plate is always full, more so in hard times than good. You see, people ain't giving money for God; they are giving it for themselves, so God will do somethin' for 'um. They too stupid to realize most of what they give goes to the preacher. Preachers were the only folks I seen ridin' around in new cars during the depression. Don't never see one ridin' in a rattle trap today either do you?"

My grandfather's influence on his children was profound. Although he had a daughter (Willa Mae) who frequented church as an adult, she was never hypocritical or judgmental. However, all three of his children generally reflected his view of religion as far too often hypocritical and too judgmental. As the old saying goes, "The apple does not fall far from the tree."

I had great respect for my grandfather, and idolized my Aunt Willa Mae, who was just as saintly, kind, caring, loving and generous as my grandmother. My Uncle Lloyd, though often like my grandfather, a man who did not suffer fools lightly and could be brutally honest about his feelings, was, like his sister, an individual respected by those who liked him and even by the few who did not like him. Now, my father, Worth Frye, and I had a sometimes difficult relationship because of his alcoholism and my perceived lack of intelligence when compared to him and his father. However, that did not alter my respect and

## The Real Jesus Seen in Black and White
## From the Resurrected Spirit of Dixon Frye

and sincere admiration for him. Worth Frye was a man who was well-known for his business acumen, sales ability, mechanical aptitude and marketing skill. Today, I reflect on the often difficult relationship we had and lay some of the blame at my grandfather's feet, because, I sincerely believe that my father often felt unloved by my dear grandfather, and after many discussions with my Aunt Willa Mae, who always had a special bond with my father, I can see, upon reflection, that my grandfather was a man whom I actually never heard utter the words, "I love you" to anyone but his daughter.

We are all partially products of our environment, and in order to understand my grandfather and how he looked at life, one must look at the unique circumstances under which he grew to manhood, and those circumstances had a lot to do with the way he looked upon religion.

He was born in 1900, and though religion has an inordinate amount of influence in the USA today, it was much more pervasive when my grandfather was a child. Being the son of an unwed mother was frowned upon in those days, and though his mom eventually married and he was adopted by her husband, he never escaped the stigma of being called a bastard by his schoolmates, and even his teachers. That was the religion by which he was tempered, the children paying for the sins of the fathers, or mothers in his case. Old Testament

J. Wayne Frye                    13

retribution and rebuke was freely practiced by the hypocrites even more so back then than it is today.

That judgmental arrogance taught children by their parents led to my grandfather having to engage in fights often to defend his honour. Finally, by the third grade, despite being highly intelligent, he simply had enough of the teasing, the judgmental arrogance and intimidation. At the age of eight, he walked in his home on the last day of school and said to his mother, "I ain't going back to no school in the fall. I'll have the same teacher next year and she looks on me as the son of the devil, and the kids all have been taught to have nothing to do with me because I am the son of a sinner. Mamma, them kids and that teacher are bigger sinners than you will ever be. Somebody ought to tell them to let he who is without sin cast the first stone."

His mother, who had always felt him a child far wiser than his years, said, "Son, you done learned more than the teacher. I don't see that they can teach you any more. You know how to fix anything, cause you been the man of the house around here ever since I can remember. I am proud of you boy, proud to call you my son, and don't pay no never mind to anybody who calls you names. You better than most of them, cause you see things different than they see 'um, and you don't need no Bible-thumper telling you how evil you are. You bout' the best boy they ever was."

**The Real Jesus Seen in Black and White
From the Resurrected Spirit of Dixon Frye**

I remember my great grandmother Frye as a woman much like her son, someone who simply did not suffer fools lightly and who never bent when facing the winds of adversity. Strength and courage were a staple for people who were poor, and lived in a nation that from its beginnings, when founded by a bunch of rich people who wanted to avoid paying taxes to England, was run by and for the wealthy. In all these years, very little has changed, as the rich and privileged get a free ride in one of the most morally and economically corrupt nations on earth. My own grandfather pointed that out to me many times this folly when he would say, "Wayne, this here country ain't nothing but a giant corporation. Been that way since the very beginning, and religion is the tool the rich use to control the poor. They keep telling us we'll get our reward in the sky in the by and by, but ain't nothing but a pack of lies."

Dixon Frye, unlike his wife and my dad had no musical talent, but he loved to recite the old Joe Hill song to me, the one Hill sang when he was getting ready to be hanged on trumped up charges brought by the mine owners in Utah as a result of his attempt to unionize the miners. I never saw my grandfather cry, but when he would recite that song; you could sense melancholia about him, as if he was feeling poor people's pain.

*Long-haired preachers come out every night
Try to tell you what's wrong and what's right*

J. Wayne Frye                                   15

**The Real Jesus Seen in Black and White**
**From the Resurrected Spirit of Dixon Frye**

*But when asked how 'bout something to eat*
*They will answer in voices so sweet*

*You will eat, bye and bye*
*In that glorious land above the sky*
*Work and pray, live on hay*
*You'll get pie in the sky when you die*

*And the Starvation Army, they play*
*And they sing and they clap and they pray*
*Till they get all your coin on the drum*
*Then they tell you when you're on the bum*

*Holy Rollers and Jumpers come out*
*And they holler, they jump and they shout*
*Give your money to Jesus, they say*
*He will cure all diseases today*
*:*
*If you fight hard for children and wife*
*Try to get something good in this life*
*You're a sinner and bad man, they tell*
*When you die you will sure go to hell.*

*Workingmen of all countries, unite*
*Side by side we for freedom will fight*
*When the world and its wealth we have gained*
*To the grafters we'll sing this refrain*

*You will eat, bye and bye*
*When you've learned how to cook and how to fry*
*Chop some wood, 'twill do you good*
*Then you'll eat in the sweet bye and bye*

J. Wayne Frye

## The Real Jesus Seen in Black and White
## From the Resurrected Spirit of Dixon Frye

I also loved to listen to him tell stories about how the Bible was used to scare people. It was because of him that I first became interested in reading the Bible, not so much to accept what I read, but to question it and, as he did, try to see through the veil of mischief used to scare people. I remember when I was much older he once told me that the real Bible didn't have hell, but that hell was simply an invention of interpreters so they could scare people.

Again, as was our custom, one night as we sat in the swing, he said to me, "Boy, depending on the Bible for truth is like expecting Republicans to actually do something for the common man. It just ain't gonna happen. I stopped believing in fairy tales when I was about five. Now don't misunderstand me, I ain't saying they never was a man named Jesus, but I am a saying that I ain't one of these god-darned fools who believes some angel named Gabriel is gonna blow his horn one day and all the people in the graveyards is gonna start kicking the lids off their coffins and start coming outta the ground. I mean come on. You tell people that is religious that you belief in flying elephants or goddesses with four heads and they laugh at you, but tell them that the rapture is coming and a host of angles will come upon the earth on judgment day and they start shouting hallelujah, amen, dancing in the church aisles and speaking in tongues. And these is people laughing at flying elephants."

## The Real Jesus Seen in Black and White
## From the Resurrected Spirit of Dixon Frye

"I ain't no smart man, but I read many a Bible in my day. I even read old, old Bibles from long ago, and they keep doctoring 'um up to get people all scared. You get your old Bibles and hell ain't never mentioned in the story of Adam and Eve. Even when Moses led people outta Egypt the old Bibles never mentioned about the Pharaoh going to hell. If you study hell in the Bible, you're in for a long, useless search for facts, definitions and explanations. Why? 'Cause the Hebrew prophets never mentioned a place where human beings are in eternal torment, gnashing their teeth forever. Nor did the prophets ever mention even the possibility of suffering after death. Ain't that odd, if there really is a hell and God wanted us to know how to avoid it? The Hebrew Bible or as you know it, the Old Testament, mentions a place called Sheol, but in Hebrew that means the grave or simply the place where good, bad and in-between dwell forever. I can't read no Hebrew. I have enough trouble reading English, but I knows how to take my mamma's old Bible down she got from her people long ago and read what was writ before somebody decided to change it."

"Now, I don't read Greek either, but I done looked up the word Hades and found out that means grave in ancient Greek or the place of the dead. So I done figured out that hell is an invention of them preachers what wants you to put money in that collection plate so you can stay outta hell. So hell ain't a biblical teaching at all,

J. Wayne Frye

**The Real Jesus Seen in Black and White
From the Resurrected Spirit of Dixon Frye**

but mistranslations used by snake oil salesmen, or as they like to call themselves - ministers of God's word - to brainwash believers into forking over their hard-earned money while obeying commandments they never bother to obey themselves. Now, them that suffers most from this tomfoolery is young children. That's why the church sends out buses to pick up children for Sunday School, so they can get 'um when they young and brainwash 'um. Children trust their parents, but parents ain't doing their jobs when they just turn their kids over to preachers and Sunday School teachers to mislead 'um. You gotta make sure your young'ins get a little common sense along with that Sunday morning preachin'. You know what boy, I believe most people get plenty of punishment in this here thing we call life, and if they's a God gonna punish you after death, I ain't so sure I wanna worship that kinda God anyway. I wanna loving God, not one who is going around handing out punishment all the time for any little thing you do wrong."

It is evident to me today that Dixon Frye had great depth of understanding, even though he was uneducated. Child abuse was rarely mentioned in my youth as taking a belt to your children was considered normal. Though I adored my grandmother, even she would, on occasion, send me to get a hickory stick to whop me across the butt once or twice as punishment. I do not hold that against her since that was considered appropriate discipline for the times. To her credit, she actually, toward the end of her life, told me that it was wrong to use physical violence in disciplining children and she said she had been wrong to do what her parents had done to her.

Why do I mention this? Simply because my grandfather, in his somewhat inarticulate way that night also told me that using the fear of hell on children was a form of child abuse. Though the words are mine, the thoughts are his. Exposing children to that type of fear is emotional, psychological and spiritual abuse. He felt that there is absolutely no reason for adults to threaten children with hell in the thinly-veiled but terrifying threat that Jesus saves, but only if you believe Christian dogma. Children grow up, a fact that eludes Christian theologians who insist that Jesus loves the little children, and yet will inexplicably turn his back on them when they reach the mysterious age of accountability, which ironically was never mentioned by Jesus, Peter, Paul, or any other apostle or prophet in regard to salvation. If Jesus never condemned anyone to hell at any age, isn't it blasphemy to threaten people with hell in God's name? This was my grandfather's philosophy.

What did all this mean to Dixon Frye? If you believe in a loving, compassionate, wise, just God, you may conclude that hell has always been either an error of translation or an outright human

**The Real Jesus Seen in Black and White**
**From the Resurrected Spirit of Dixon Frye**

fabrication. Why would human beings invent hell? Well, as my grandfather saw it, religion was all about control. It was a dandy way to increase church attendance, and above all, to keep those collection plates full. I remember he once said, "Wayne, them preachers get little kids to put in their quarters in that collection plate, and them kids do it cause they think it's what Jesus wants. Them quarters amount to a lot of money. And when them kids get to be adults, they start putting in dollar bills which is even more money for those hate spewing hypocrites."

While most people were praising Oral Roberts and Billy Graham back in those days, my grandfather was saying, "Those two are raking in millions off people's stupidity. People actually believe those two can pray 'um into heaven. That somehow those two are holier than they are. Let me tell you somethin', your grandmother's got more of God in her little finger than them boys got in their whole bodies."

Jesus applauded the compassion of the Good Samaritan, a man of the wrong religion who practiced compassion. Will all the good Samaritans go to hell? Will Jesus fail to practice what he preached and not be a Good Samaritan himself? Will he condemn the saints of other religions to eternal torture: Gandhi, the great man of peace, for instance? Are he and Buddha going to be in hell along with Lord Krishna?

## The Real Jesus Seen in Black and White
## From the Resurrected Spirit of Dixon Frye

My grandfather was what he, himself, called "a pot-bellied stove Bible scholar," as he would often sit around the stove with others and destroy their arguments for believing in what he called fairy tales. His knowledge of the Bible rivalled any Harvard Divinity School scholar, and though he might not have been as articulate as they were, he, in his simple way, could deliver cogent, concise, perceptive arguments that often disarmed the most stellar of believers.

I can remember he once was in the house he and my grandmother had given away when they closed the general store and moved to a nearby town. He listened to the minister, who was there for dinner and was pontificating on how those who did not know Jesus would burn in hell, even the little children in backward countries. My grandfather, who loved to show how much disrespect he had for those who displayed a superior attitude and arrogance, said, "You need to read your Bible preacher. Jesus got baptised by John the Baptist, but he never said anything about babies being baptised. Neither did Paul or the other apostles. These teachings were only introduced when the church figured out fear of hell was a powerful way to control people. If Jesus loved children and they were in danger of going to hell once they reached a certain age, or if they weren't splashed with holy water, how could he have failed to tell his disciples exactly what needed to be done to save them? Truth is there was no hell at the time Jesus

J. Wayne Frye

# The Real Jesus Seen in Black and White
## From the Resurrected Spirit of Dixon Frye

and Paul were preaching and there ain't no hell today. How could a loving, wise, just Jesus never once mention its creation and purpose to any of his prophets or apostles? How could God cause or allow billions of people to suffer for all eternity when they died knowing nothing about the Bible, Jesus or hell? Why would God save the chosen few by grace, but deny any chance of grace to billions of people who never heard of Jesus? I tell you what preacher; I don't want no part of that kinda God. Hell was developed after Jerusalem was destroyed and the Christian church reborn in Greece and Rome, where people believed in the hell of the pagan religions. By that time Jesus and Paul were no longer here in the flesh, to stand agin the witchdoctors who were trying to scare people. Well, I ain't a man who scares easy. None of you hell-fire and damnation preachers are ever gonna scare me."

The minister, my grandmother, my great aunt, great uncle and my two second cousins sat in shock at how my grandfather had brought the minister's arrogance tumbling down like the tower of Babble. The minister also sat in silence, and I, a small child, was filled with pride that I could call such a wise man, grandfather. Though I often looked upon him with trepidation due to his towering physical stature and his sometimes gruff manner, I sat at that kitchen table swelling with admiration that night. Here was a man of great wisdom I thought.

## The Real Jesus Seen in Black and White
## From the Resurrected Spirit of Dixon Frye

My grandfather's scholarly knowledge of the Bible motivated me to read it time and time again, and I would often discuss it with my grandparents. I have never lost my fascination with the Bible, and have probably read it cover to cover no less than two dozen times in my lifetime. My grandmother was more devout than my grandfather, and though she questioned the cruelty of the Bible, she was more accepting of it than he was. He and she both saw the Bible as not being infallible. I can remember my grandmother saying, "How can you believe that, as the Bible says, you should stone children for being stubborn; commit murder against those not considered God fearing, killing even babies; and to kill mature women then take their virgin daughters as sex slaves?" Then my grandfather would offer with great disdain, "And what about selling your daughter to the highest bidder? Wonder what Willa Mae would think of that?"

My grandfather never wavered in his belief that religion brought more woe to the world than joy. He saw religion as a sinister method of control that kept people in mental bondage and trapped them in economic servitude to the moneyed class; although, he never would have articulated it that way. Most of all, he was a man who practiced common sense, and he was just unable to believe in angels fluttering around and in an evil being with horns reigning over an underworld where people would burn forever, paying for their sins.

## The Real Jesus Seen in Black and White
## From the Resurrected Spirit of Dixon Frye

My grandfather did not view all ministers and religious people with disdain. In fact, he was quick to praise the many that were not closed minded and did not cloak themselves in self-righteous arrogance. He might disagree with their belief in what he termed fairy-tales, but he respected them for their commitment to kindness, acceptance and justice. In fact, he had many clergymen who were his friends and they held him in high regard. He even attended church in what I and my cousins referred to as "down in the country." There was a small country church near his old general store and he and my grandmother had a strong affinity for that place of worship as it was a strong link to their past and to the place they had called home for so many years. It was also the place where the annual Hopkins Reunion was held every year, as my grandmother's mother was a Hopkins. It was at one of those reunions where I saw my grandfather do something totally out of character. Praying was something I never saw him do except for that one time. As the gathered crowd was saying a prayer for one of the Hopkins' youth who had contracted cancer, my grandfather, as the probably two hundred people gathered there were bowing their heads, whispered, "If 'un you exist Lord, keep my children safe from this horrible disease."

I reached over, took his hand and squeezed hard. I got tears in my eyes, because he was a hard man with a soft heart and terribly humble.

### The Real Jesus Seen in Black and White
### From the Resurrected Spirit of Dixon Frye

Each moment with my grandfather was an exercise in learning, because even the most mundane thing, I learned later in life, was an opportunity to acquire knowledge and observe the world with a critical eye. Looking back on it now, I can see that the reason his children were so successful in life was because he taught them to think for themselves and never turn their minds over to pontificating, bombastic, hate-spewing minions of despair.

J. Wayne Frye

## CHAPTER 2
## TASTE HIS KNOWLEDGE

Dixon Frye would probably be very appreciative and supportive of this book which I believe represents what he stood for when it came to religion. The title reflects the spirit of a man who saw the intrinsic evil of those who want to control all thought and make mankind march, not forward, but to stay trapped in the past where adherence to a code of conduct defined by self-appointed protectors of public morals makes all of humanity slaves to a thick black book filled with cruelty.

The purpose of this book is not to offend anyone, but rather to get those with open minds to reflect and give serious thought to how religion, especially in the USA and the Muslim world, is used to ridicule, condemn and trap people in the grasp of those who would label everything according to the dictates the Bible (or Koran) which traps people in a world of fairy tales and

## The Real Jesus Seen in Black and White
## From the Resurrected Spirit of Dixon Frye

heaps the wrath of their evil God upon all who diverge from what they define as the righteous path. The world can never move forward as long as religion is allowed to trap people in an archaic stranglehold that will not allow mankind free-thought. The right-wing Christians of America are every bit as dangerous as the miscreants of the Middle East who want to march man backward to the Dark Ages. Even a staunch conservative like Barry Goldwater had this to say about the right wing Christians as far back as 1964: "Mark my word; if and when these preachers get control of the Republican Party, and they're sure trying to do so, it's going to be a terrible damn problem. Frankly, these people frighten me. Politics and governing demand compromise, but these Christians believe they are acting in the name of God, so they can't and won't compromise. I know, I've tried to deal with them."

Goldwater was something that doesn't exist today, a conservative willing to compromise and who has compassion for the poor. He believed in the separation of church and state, because he was a fervent believer in the Constitution which enshrined that belief. He said, "Government must stand fast against the religious psychopaths who want to crush the Constitution under their jack-booted arrogance and self-righteousness while saying they honour it. The religious factions have, throughout history, tried to impose their will on others."

28        J. Wayne Frye

## The Real Jesus Seen in Black and White
## From the Resurrected Spirit of Dixon Frye

Of the religious icon of conservative thought, Jerry Falwell, he said, "Every good Christian should line up and kick Falwell's ass."

Oh, and what conservative today would dare say what he did, "Every woman has a right to control her own body, and that includes abortion."

My grandfather, though the words are mine, believed that there is no position on which people are so immovable as their religious beliefs. There is no more powerful ally one can claim in a debate than Jesus Christ, or God, or Allah, or whatever one calls this Supreme Being. But like any powerful weapon, the use of God's name on one's behalf should be used sparingly. The religious factions do not use their religious clout with wisdom. They try to force government leaders into following their position 100 percent. If you disagree with these religious groups on a particular moral issue, they complain, they threaten with a loss of money or votes or both. This was the moral hypocrisy that grated on my grandfather his entire short life of only 56 years.

He was sick and tired of the political preachers across America telling citizens that if you want to be a moral person, you must believe in *A, B, C* and *D*. "Just who do these arrogant jerks think they are," he used to say. Then he would continue, "They actually believe they are communicating with God? What arrogance."

## The Real Jesus Seen in Black and White
## From the Resurrected Spirit of Dixon Frye

My grandfather used to look at television preachers with me on Sunday mornings and say, "Wayne, you want to learn marketing, study these clowns. These guys are better than any salesman I ever seen. They are selling sacks of cow manure and the suckers line up to buy the sacks. They get rich off people's stupidity. One million, three million, five million – they brag about it. I don't believe in that. It's not a very religious thing to do."

This book is an attempt to look at what is happening in regards to the growing religious theocracy in America today and explore what some of the reactions of my grandfather would be. Though he has been dead for many years, his perceptive view of religion is as valid today as it was all those years ago. So, let's get started.

While writing this book, a Muslim terrorist attack killed well over 100 people in Paris. The first thing my grandfather would have said, after criticizing George Bush and Dick Cheney for being the architects who created the ISIS terrorist group with their lies about Iraq and WMD, would have been to categorically find fault with all religion. I can recall he once said to me about fundamentalist Christians, "these crazy rapture waiting nuts are a plague on humanity. They are worse than the flu that spreads its virus among people, and like the flu there seems to be absolutely no cure, because they will not take any dose of common sense."

The two of us were walking in the woods behind his house, and I looked up at the trees and the sunlight peeking through the towering trees and said, "God sure made this a beautiful place didn't he?" He replied, "Well, don't know whether God made it or not, but it is beautiful yes, but remember that even ugly things can hold beauty, son. The cactus ain't a pretty plant. In fact, it is down right ugly and if you touch it you'll get pricked, but if you lost in the desert and are thirsty, you can cut into it and find moisture, life-saving cactus juice to quench your thirst. And beautiful things can be very deadly. The oleander is a beautiful flower, but it harbours poison. You see, religion offers lots of beauty, but it is also filled with ugliness. You just said God made all this. Well, religious people think he made this in six days despite what science says about the earth. Now, I ain't got nothing agin' religion until it starts telling me that the earth is flat or that I need to pray to get over a sickness rather than go the doctor. If un' I need my appendix out, I don't need God, I need a good surgeon."

As a writer I often use flowery language and depend on a thesaurus for aid in finding just the right word to use, but in his simple, uneducated use of language, my grandfather was actually much more eloquent than I am when it came to descriptively painting a picture with words.

## The Real Jesus Seen in Black and White
## From the Resurrected Spirit of Dixon Frye

Dixon Frye saw religion as totally irrational. One day we were riding to Clyde Steed's Texaco Service Station to get my favourite treat, Buttercup Chocolate Ice Cream. On the way I said, "How come there is so much hate in the world Granddaddy?" Well, that opened up a flood gate of philosophical musings on religion.

"Boy, one word can describe most of the hate," he said with a shrug of his shoulders. Now, he rarely used profanity in front of me, but that day it slipped out. "Goddamn religion!"

He realized he had let profanity slip out and looked a bit ashamed, but continued. "Religion is like a contagious disease. It spreads its ugliness far more than its beauty. You see, most people struck by this disease simply can't be cured, cause they refuse to take the pill of reason. They are all unreasonable, unwilling to open they's minds. The few that are reasonable get drowned out by the fanatics – those that is so wrapped up in Jesus that they won't listen, won't compromise on anything. They think having God on they's side makes them special. Ain't nothing special 'bout people who won't use they's brains. You can't have a calm conversation with people shouting amen and hallelujah. They done closed they's minds and nothing you do will make them be reasonable. They don't want no conversation. They only want you to agree with 'um, 'cause they knows they's right."

## The Real Jesus Seen in Black and White
## From the Resurrected Spirit of Dixon Frye

Looking with intensity at him, I said, "So, they just want you to agree with them, not question what they believe?"

"That is right son, absolutely right. Wars are fought over religion. This here country went to war in Europe twice and both times we knew God was on our side. Funny thing is the countries we was fightin' also thought God was on their side. Now, since we won, the religious folks believe God got us the victory. A lot of fine boys sure had to die so God could get his victory. I don't think God had nothing to do with it. I think our soldiers is the ones who done it, not God. As far as I can see, we never won that Korean War, so where was God then? The religious folks would blame it on our sinning. They'd say that we deserted God, so he deserted us. Kind of a two-faced God if he done that and what about the other side? Them communists don't even believe in God and they fought us to a standstill. I believe that Jesus was agin' war anyway, but seems like they always fightin' wars in his name."

Typical of a child, as we pulled up at Clyde Steed's Texaco, I forgot all about the profundity of our discussion and said, "Yippee, Buttercup."

Of course, today I look back upon that discussion and many others and am thankful for a grandfather who lovingly guided me and showed me how be an independent thinker.

## The Real Jesus Seen in Black and White
## From the Resurrected Spirit of Dixon Frye

When Barrack Obama was elected President in 2008, conservative Americans were traumatized as never before. Having a black man in the White House was a blow that many of them simply never got over. Ironically, Obama was not 100% black, but rather a Mulatto, as his mother was white. Still, the inherent bigotry of so many reared its ugly head continuously, though they tried to cover it up by calling him a Muslim, a communist, a non-native American, etc... However, the base problem for a large majority of the Obama haters was beneath the surface racism that boiled within the caldron of hatred that was often fanned by religious fervour. After all, separation of the races was preached to me as a child as being part of God's plan. He turned people black because of their sins. He sent them off to Africa out of disgust. This was Christian doctrine.

Of course, for many of the Obama haters, it was not racism, but the mere fact that a Democrat was in the White House. As is so often the case, Americans elect a Democrat to clean up the mess made by Republicans who are there to serve the corporations and the rich. Their policies have traditionally led to economic malaise as evidenced by every Republican elected President since 1920. Still, the middle class and many of the poor continuously vote against their own self-interest, especially since the 1950's when Republicans began to play the race card in the south, where Democrats had predominated since the Civil War,

## The Real Jesus Seen in Black and White
## From the Resurrected Spirit of Dixon Frye

and bandied the fear that the Democrats might take their precious guns. Then, in the 1960's, they learned to play the ace of all cards – religion. Yes, they became the party that loved Jesus. Though none of their actions were ever Jesus-like, the poor fell for the Svengali-like manipulation that somehow convinced them to vote against their own self-interest because Republicans loved Jesus.

My grandfather had an inarticulate way of saying it, but he saw the follies of people voting against their self-interest. He never tired of saying, "Name me one goddamn thing them 'publicans ever done for the common man – just one."

I was never privileged to sit in my grandfathers' general store until long after he was dead, but I visited my cousin in 1999 who had resurrected the small, run-down store as he was living in the house where my grandparents had lived before moving to Asheboro, North Carolina. As we walked over to the store that was maybe a 100 feet away from the house I noticed the old well where my grandfather had taken a sip of water from a dipper handed to him by my grandmother who captured his heart the very first time he saw her. We stopped. My cousin Kirby wound the bucket down and brought up some cool water for me to drink. I looked over at the old tree where my great grandfather was tied after he blamed himself for a mine disaster that killed several men and the guilt drove him crazy. They would tie him there during the day for fear he would run off. That old place seemed to be alive with the spirit of my long gone grandfather whom I was beginning to admire and appreciate more as I aged.

As we sat around the remains of an old cracker barrel he had saved, and my cousin Kirby sighed and said, "Wayne, your granddaddy was a remarkable man. People around here still talk about him and he's been dead over 40 years now. That man left a lasting legacy that has been passed on one generation to the other."

My cousin is gone now, and soon the old house and rickety old store will, no doubt, be razed. A bit of history will finally be ploughed under, but the person who owns it is a farmer, a Hopkins relative. So, on that hallowed ground will grow crops to feed people, just as my grandfather fed the needy who wandered by during the depression. Perhaps a bit of him will live on as people sit down at their tables for a meal and taste the food raised on that farm that marks the spot where a remarkable man lived. I am so grateful that I was able to taste his knowledge for the first twelve years of my life.

## CHAPTER 3
## HE KNOWS MORE THAN I DO

*The real evil in the world is ignorance.*
*Religion is used to keep people ignorant.*
*Keep people afraid so they will obey.*
*I may not be educated, but I ain't ignorant,*
*And that really riles up them Bible-Thumpers.*
...............................................Dixon Frye

All it takes for a collapse of common sense is for ignorance to start serving evil. Ignorance is the first step towards becoming an employee of dark forces, and in a large part of the world today, especially in the USA and the Middle East, religion is not a force for the light, but for the darkness. My grandfather saw that long ago, and he made sure that his three children were able to see through the darkness of ignorance, and thankfully, for twelve years of my young life, he showed me a light that has been a beacon to guide me through the stormy seas of life in a world that prefers ignorance to enlightenment.

## The Real Jesus Seen in Black and White
## From the Resurrected Spirit of Dixon Frye

Andrew Werner is a Biblical scholar whom I read and his trysts on religion seem to come right from the mouth of my grandfather. I often wonder if he did not meet him somewhere long ago. He says, "Religion is man's invention, and he probably makes his religion proportional to his development." So, I share his manifest within what follows, and as I said, it is pure Dixon Frye.

I gave up on America in 2003 mostly because of what I saw as a coming calamity caused by people ignorant enough to elect George Bush President, although his first term was an appointment by the Supreme Court, as the majority of the people actually voted against him, but because of an archaic electoral system and a 5-4 Republican majority on the Supreme Court, Bush wound up on Pennsylvania Avenue. However, my second reason for leaving was what I saw as a growing theocracy in America. Despite the election of Barrack Obama in 2008, it did not seem to subside. In fact, I think it has been solidified in response to his election, as the religious bigots rallied in masse against him. The vitriol and hatred matched nothing I had ever seen before in the USA in regards to a politician. He was portrayed by the religious right wing nuts as the anti-Christ. In fact, the bacon eating, beer drinking Obama was branded a Muslim by the hate mongers who gave up on proving he was not born in America and moved to other means to question his Americanism.

## The Real Jesus Seen in Black and White
## From the Resurrected Spirit of Dixon Frye

From this hatred sprung a long list of Republicans who used this racism, fear and religious dogma to their political advantage. Demagoguery is alive and well in the Republican Party. In fact, it is at the very core of all the people they put up for office. It is almost as if hypocrisy is a requirement to seek office as a Republican. In my opinion, none of them actually believe the malarkey they spew out to the American people. They are simply playing on people's ignorance. My grandfather would have had a field day with today's Republicans.

Though I shall use my own words and some of Werner's, I am parroting what my grandfather taught me with what follows in regards to the purpose of religion. My words are perhaps more flowery than his, but I wish I had recorded his words so that I could have put them here completely in tact, as ultimately, his simple way of saying things was far superior in eloquence.

Religion, according to Dixon, is designed to focus the people's attention and energy on a single, unchanging, uncompromising and invisible supreme being who allegedly created an inferior human race just for some extra companionship and love for himself and then supposedly foisted a set of oppressive, almost impossible to comprehend and in some cases arbitrary rules on them, which if broken would be met with unimaginable punishment. Fear is the

## The Real Jesus Seen in Black and White
## From the Resurrected Spirit of Dixon Frye

chief element in keeping people in line, as followers are in a continuing state of trepidation and compliance. They are afraid to question the intentions of this invisible being and they are afraid of even expressing their own individuality in many cases. Christians and other religions, with a few exceptions, teach that the individual has virtually no power to do anything except pray, worship and plead with God to not send them to the fires of hell. At this point, my grandfather would often shake his head and chuckle at how gullible people were. In fact, he referred to it not as gullibility, but as desperation. Most people, as Oscar Wilde said, *lead lives of quiet desperation.*

Believers are taught to practice self denial and are told that their own will is totally irrelevant. Religious followers believe that they are yielding their will to a benevolent cosmic individual who has single-handedly created the whole universe and has their best interests at heart. Along the way to this nirvana that awaits them in the hereafter, they are to allow interpreters of this God's word to control their lives while they pop money into a collection plate to furnish these interpreters with a lavish lifestyle, while, for many of the givers, life is a constant struggle. Of course, they all are anticipatory of that great place up in the sky in the sweet bye and bye when they will get their reward without asking why the few are entitled to those rewards here on

**The Real Jesus Seen in Black and White**
**From the Resurrected Spirit of Dixon Frye**

earth. Question not God's will, just accept it as he knows what is best for you. Again, at this point my grandfather would usually say, "As I always tell the preachers who are telling me how to get right with God, if God or one of those wing-flapping angels whispers it to me, I'll listen to his advice, but I don't see you wearing no halo or flapping no wings."

My grandfather had particular disdain for Catholic Bishops whom he saw on television in their expensive fancy silk garments. He once told me when a bishop came to town riding in a limousine. "Boy, you ever think about how many hungry people could be fed with what the church spends on his clothes, that car and the chauffeur to drive him around? I don't think you'd ever see Jesus in fancy clothes or riding in a limousine. People is plum crazy handing over their money, their will and freedoms to these hypocrites."

It appeared to my grandfather that religion constantly degraded and humiliated its followers in order to glorify God. He felt many people were eager to give away their power to authority and seemed to have a need and even a desire to be ruled and disciplined by it. He always said that it was because most people were too stupid to make their own decisions, so they turned it over to somebody else, and that the world was full of somebody else's to take your money and do your thinking for you.

J. Wayne Frye                                41

## The Real Jesus Seen in Black and White
## From the Resurrected Spirit of Dixon Frye

He saw religion as appealing to primitive, superstitious and weak minded people. For him, it had no place in the 20th century. Once, as I was sitting in his car, riding back from Clyde Steed's with my Buttercup ice cream in my hand, shovelling it in my mouth with glee, I said, "Granddaddy, why does God let us suffer so much? Seems kind of funny that he is supposed to be so loving and then he lets all these bad things happen."

"The reason we have life in this world is to experience life in this world, not to spend our entire lives studying an old book filled with cruelty in the first half as God sends down terror to punish people. The second half of the book ain't too bad, as it teaches us to not judge others, to be compassionate, to help our neighbours. They took most of the fear out of the book with Jesus, but they won't throw away that first part unfortunately, and that is where the trouble mostly comes from. Of course, this Jesus tale has been manipulated by preachers and others so they benefit from it, too. Best thing you can do in life boy is never accept what anybody tells you without checking the facts, and that goes for believing everything your granddaddy tells you too. I ain't perfect," then he got a smile on his face and continued, "Well, almost perfect maybe. Me and Jesus is pretty close to perfect." We had a grand laugh together, and looking back, that was one of my best childhood moments ever.

J. Wayne Frye

## The Real Jesus Seen in Black and White
## From the Resurrected Spirit of Dixon Frye

When I got older, my grandfather discussed things with a commitment to making me think more. As we were sitting in the living room one evening after watching *Amos and Andy* on television, which was a show that used stereotyped African Americans as main characters, I asked him why it seemed like coloured folks (the common term at the time) were made fun of on television, and why the church didn't try to teach people to be less bigoted.

He seemed to think long and hard as he let out a sigh. There was a silence that permeated the room for about a minute, and then he said. "Wayne, I am prejudiced myself. I come up in the south and we's all taught that somehow the coloured man ain't our equal, and it is even religion that teaches that. We are told in church people are black 'cause of sin. God sent people who built the tower of Babble to other lands, made them all speak different languages cause of sin, and he turned them different colours, but, of course, he made the white man better according to southerners. Now, you and me knows that is a bunch of horse pucky. Still, I find myself being less kind to the coloureds. It's wrong and I work on it ever day, but I got a far piece to go before I lick it. I think maybe because of your grandmother you done licked it, and I gotta do my best to overcome what I was taught by my parents, kin-folks and the church."

## The Real Jesus Seen in Black and White
## From the Resurrected Spirit of Dixon Frye

Amos and Andy came on at 8:00 PM and my grandfather was usually in bed promptly every night by 7:30 or 8:00, but this night he was in a talkative mood. I felt that I had opened an avenue of discussion that would broaden my knowledge by picking the brains of a man I was growing to admire more and more. I blurted out, "Granddaddy, do you believe in Jesus?"

Again, there was a silence in the room as he seemed in deep thought. Then, he said, "Can't say as I do or as I don't. You know there may have been a fine and gentle man named Jesus, but was he the son of God? Well, you and me both knows that making up stories is a favourite practice of the religious types. It is a mighty good story I have to say, but is it true? Well, I have hard time believing in angels and the devil or all that other stuff that seems like fairy tales, so believing that story ain't really easy. I mean it is still all about guilt, trying to make us take the blame for a man being crucified that we didn't even know. He died for my sins? I mean I ain't all that bad, so why I need somebody to be crucified for me? I can make up for my sins by trying to correct them and not do 'um agin. I mean here we go agin with all that guilt. The believers are then so grateful that they have been saved by the son of God nearly 2000 years before they were born that in some cases they throw away all reason and good judgment to obey and worship this God and his son."

## The Real Jesus Seen in Black and White
## From the Resurrected Spirit of Dixon Frye

"Well, let's look at this thing with some sense Wayne. We supposed to believe that this God who went around killing innocent men, women and children in the Old Testament, raining down plagues and pestilence, all of a sudden decides to send his only son to help us, only to see his son get tortured and murdered, and then instead of unleashing all this wrath he used before, simply forgives us from all crimes past and present, just don't sound like the God I read about in the Old Testament. Why'd he change all of a sudden?"

At the time, I was mystified and intrigued. Today, what is the lesson in the discussion I had that night? Again, in my words, not his, I believe that my grandfather saw religion as mass psychological enslavement and disempowerment. I believe he saw the whole God thing as a story concocted by the religious elites for the purpose of controlling the masses. If there is a prime creator in this universe, why would he need and demand our frivolous worship and blind obedience. Neither of those things requires any level of mental aptitude or creativity. In fact, it lacks any of the elements of a clear thinking person. Tell the average Christian that Buddha was, like Jesus, born of a virgin and he will laugh and scoff at your impertinence to even suggest someone else was born of a virgin. The Christian refuses to entertain any logical thought. It is his glorified exaltation of the Jesus way or the highway. That attitude is not Jesus-like at all.

## The Real Jesus Seen in Black and White
## From the Resurrected Spirit of Dixon Frye

Tell people the story of the Greek God Prometheus, which is almost word-for-word the story of Jesus right up to the crucifixion, and was recorded thousands of years before Jesus, and the Christian refuses to even entertain the thought that the Bible could have retold ancient stories but substituted other times and names. Even the story of the end of the world by flood was told many times before it popped up in the Bible. Inquiring minds would seek out knowledge, but knowledge means you have to think, and people need to cling to hope that there is something after this life, because most people have little hope in this life.

Jesus is a super hero. Heroes are important to people, because it makes them feel that individuals can rise to the occasion. For example, only in America would they make a hero out of someone like Chris Kyle, a sniper who killed hundreds of Muslims, including women and children. What is heroic about lying in wait, hidden from view and in relative safety while targeting people with a high powered rifle? Would not a hero actually confront his adversary, rather than hiding from view. Chris Kyle was no hero. A hero is someone who puts his life on the line to save someone. All Chris Kyle did was support the lies and manipulative manifestations of the criminals George W. Bush and Dick Cheney. Real heroes would have handed those jerks their rifles and said, "If this war is so noble

## The Real Jesus Seen in Black and White
## From the Resurrected Spirit of Dixon Frye

let your children come over here and do the fighting. Let's watch some of the privileged class do a little dying for a change."

Religion is like a drug, and the drug for Christians is this 2000 year old hero. The churches don't permit their followers to have any real truth and knowledge because that would empower the people too much, so they spoon feed them fairy tales that the poor, helpless, desperate creatures sop up like gravy with a biscuit called Jesus. Pope Leo the 10th said, "How well we know what a profitable superstition this fable of Christ has been for us and our predecessors." It is a statement the church suppressed for years, because it was obvious that even the pope did not believe in the story of Jesus. He also intonated that most people long to be dominated and controlled and to believe that there is some evil boogie man out there they must be protected from. He saw most people as simple-minded children who were easily manipulated. Many years later, one of the pope's advisors said, "Jesus is Santa Claus for adults."

After all these centuries people still haven't learned to think for themselves. They need some spiritual guru to provide them with guidance. The profitable televangelist business is predicated on the simple fact that people will not do research, will not seek out truth, but allow others to tell them what the truth is.

## The Real Jesus Seen in Black and White
## From the Resurrected Spirit of Dixon Frye

I, for example, as a child always believed that Adam and Eve were the first people. However, my Bible scholar grandfather told me one day, "No, no son, Adam had a wife before Eve. It is in the accounts rendered in the Old Bibles. Those accounts were suppressed by the church for fear it would make people think the story of Adam and Eve was false. Her name was Lilith. Let me relate you the story as I once read it in an ancient Bible. The angels who are in charge of medicine were Snvi, Snsvi, and Smnglof. After God created Adam, who was alone, he said *it is not good for man to be alone*. He then created a woman for Adam, from the earth, as he had created Adam himself, and called her Lilith. Adam and Lilith began to fight. Now, you are old enough to know about sex, so you will understand when I tell you that Lilith said she would not lie on the bottom, but would get on top. However, Adam told her she was fit only to be in the bottom position, as God made man the superior person. Lilith responded that they were equal to each other since they were both created from the earth."

At this point I began to laugh at the preposterousness of the whole story, but my grandfather said, "This really ain't funny boy, because the world is full of people who don't know about this story but they believe the other ridiculous things in the Bible. You just getting old enough to understand how ridiculous all this baloney is. But people actually believe this stuff."

## The Real Jesus Seen in Black and White
## From the Resurrected Spirit of Dixon Frye

I could not resist saying, "But Granddaddy, how can anybody believe this silliness? Angel's with medicine. Did they run a drug store in heaven? God making people out of earth. People would laugh at me if I said I believed in Santa Claus, but they expect me to believe this?"

"I know boy. I know. Don't make no sense."

"OK Granddaddy, so tell me the rest of the story. I can't wait until next Bible class in school." (Yes, we had Bible in public school in those days.)

Seemingly pleased that I was questioning the authenticity of the sacred Bible, he continued with an intense gleam in his eyes. "Lilith grew tired of Adam's arrogance and flew away into the thin air. Adam stood in prayer before almighty God and said that the woman he had made for him ran away. At once, God sent these three angels to bring her back. He told Adam if she agrees to come back, fine. If not she must permit one hundred of her children to die every day." Granddaddy gave me a little wink as he said, "Obviously she and Adam had been pretty busy and not too concerned about who was on top or bottom if she had that many children."

We both laughed out loud, as the preposterousness of having hundreds of children was beyond any human possibility, but this was the Bible, so what could one expect?

## The Real Jesus Seen in Black and White
## From the Resurrected Spirit of Dixon Frye

"Anyway, these angels left God and chased Lilith. They found her in the sea, in the mighty waters where the Egyptians would later be drowned when chasing Moses. They told her God's word, but she did not wish to return. The angels told her they would drown her."

We both were laughing with some regularity now, but I could tell my grandfather was enjoying telling the story, as he continued. "So, she told them to leave her alone and she agreed to have 100 of her children die every day. They did not drown her but went back and told God what happened. Kind of funny ain't it that a being who is supposed to know everything had to be told by angels what Lilith said. Anyway, God decided to make another woman while also killing 100 of Lilith's children every day. He did not make this other woman from earth, but from one of Adam's ribs. Thus came along Eve, who obviously was willing to be on the bottom."

We both burst out laughing as my grandmother walked in. She got a disgusted look on her face and said, "Dixon, you talking about sex with that boy?"

Granddaddy said, "Yep, and he knows more than I do."

**The Real Jesus Seen in Black and White**
**From the Resurrected Spirit of Dixon Frye**

# CHAPTER 4
# THE GRAND STAGE OF LIFE

*Maybe Jesus was a real person.*
*Perhaps he did take on the Roman Empire.*
*Hey, if he was real, he set a good example.*
*He could have died on the cross.*
*Resurrected? I don't think so.*
*When you dead, you dead, boy.*
*Now, people are afraid of death.*
*So they need to believe things don't just end.*
*People just naturally are easy to scare.*
*There it is again - fear.*
*Yep, fear is what gives the church control.*
.............................................Dixon Frye

My grandfather and I were probably closer that night than at anytime in our lives, save for the time he rescued me from a rattle snake. There are times when we genuinely realize we are loved, and though my grandfather never said he loved me, not even once, there was an incident that still

## The Real Jesus Seen in Black and White
## From the Resurrected Spirit of Dixon Frye

pops into my mind regularly that makes me realize that a single incident, an unexpected occurrence can forever alter the feelings you have toward someone for good or bad. When I was about 6 or 7, I was walking across the vacant lot next to my grandfather's house to visit a neighbourhood friend. Suddenly, there in front of me was a huge rattle snake that was coiled to strike with its rattle beating the rhythm of death in my young mind. I screamed and my grandfather and Uncle Lloyd ran toward me with haste as I stood frozen with fear. My grandfather stopped and motioned for my uncle to do the same as they did not want to scare the rattler into striking instantly at me. My grandfather motioned for my uncle to work his way behind the rattler, which he cautiously did. My grandfather whispered for me to stand perfectly still. Suddenly my uncle, who had on work boots, moved within a foot of the rattler, raised his boot and began to stomp on it viscously. Perhaps I should heap praise on my uncle who probably took the greater risk, but it was my grandfather who swept me up into his massive arms and squeezed me tightly as I cried uncontrollably. He patted me gently on the back as he pulled me closer and closer to him, trying to assuage my fear. He said, "It's OK Wayne. Me and Lloyd will always be here to protect you no matter how old you are." My Uncle Lloyd came up and placed his hand on my back, gently patting me and said, "Hey, your grandfather and me love you, and we'll take care of you. Don't cry."

## The Real Jesus Seen in Black and White
## From the Resurrected Spirit of Dixon Frye

As I said, my grandfather never once told me he loved me, but when Uncle Lloyd said they loved me, my grandfather said, "That's right." I hugged him and felt safe and warm in his huge, muscular arms. This was love, real love. He did not have to say it. I felt it.

Worshipping is something I did willingly, but not necessarily Jesus. For example, I worshipped my father. In fact, he was like a God to me, despite our often troubled relationship. My admiration for him never wavered. He would often call me dumb, never seemed to have time for me and psychologically abused me and my mother. Still, I could never muster hate for him. In his own way, he was a living legend in the South and many other places. Being his son was not easy, because I had so much to live up to. In fact, that is why I left North Carolina when it came time for university. I had to get out from under the long shadow of success that he cast.

Then, there was my grandmother, with whom I had a special bond that melded us together all our lives. Maybe it was because she felt great compassion for me because my father was a man who rarely had time for me, and spent more time chasing women, drinking and making money than with me. It always seemed I was one of his lower priorities. If it sounds like I carry a grudge against my father, well, I do. It is something I have been working on though for many years now since he died. Still, I never felt loved by him, and maybe I understand him better now as I think the years have tempered my harsh judgement of him, as I see him as a person who also thought his own father did not love him. Though this is a book about my grandfather's religious perceptions, I cannot divorce the story from the family itself and how all of us for good or bad are tempered by the environment in which we are reared. The people who have the most profound influence on us are family members, and as time passes, I appreciate my grandfather more and more, and also my father.

It is said that love is understanding, and yet no one really understands what love of God is. How can you love something or someone whom you can neither understand nor carry on a two-way conversation with? "Hello God, hello. Wayne to God, come-in please." When I was young, I always used to attribute lack of communication from God with the fact that my problems paled in comparison to the problems of most people. So, maybe God was just too busy to be concerned with my miniscule problems.

Love and worship are also about admiration, adoration and gratitude, but how can one feel these things towards someone whom they have never seen or spent time with? Praying to that great deity in the sky might be considered spending time with God, but it is a one way relationship. All the times I have tried to talk to God, I simply never got a response. Were my prayers answered by him? Well, sometimes I did get what I asked for, but most times I didn't, especially all the times I asked God when I was a teenager to make Carolyn Lassiter like me. Oh, how many times did I plead with him to make this girl, who was one year older than I am, just give me one glance of recognition? Alas, I never had that prayer answered. O.K., maybe I was expecting too much. Hey, she was beautiful beyond compare, so what would she want with a gangly, shy boy who had no real finesse with the opposite sex? Anyway, maybe she was asking God for someone else while I was asking him for her, so perhaps God simply was confused about what to do. Of course, how many times have we heard, "God doesn't answer your prayer because he knows what is best for you." O.K. God, thanks for never letting me get just one kiss from Carolyn. That would have been awful I am sure. Maybe I would have caught the flu from her?

Worshipping a deity is nothing more than an ego based need to make one feel useful to a God who otherwise probably has no real use for anything man has to offer. And why would a God create man? Hey, he has superhuman angels to hang out with. Isn't it a bit egomaniacal to create an entity just so you can send him or her to hell if they displease you? Is that not the height of cruelty? Would an all powerful creator make a

## The Real Jesus Seen in Black and White
## From the Resurrected Spirit of Dixon Frye

dysfunctional bunch of humans just for the purpose of being worshipped? Why then give us intelligence, free choice, diversity, individuality and a strong will and then threaten to disown or terminate us as soon as we try to use them? I am not writing this book just out of respect for my grandfather, but as a catalyst for thought. People need to face the realities of life and stop living in a fantasy world created by those who want to exercise control. The United States of America is one of the most repressed societies in the world, and its citizens are seemingly incapable of independent thought because of religion.

If a single true God does exist, then creating a race of selfish, sinful, ignorant, arrogant, egotistical, money hungry and sex obsessed beings for the sole purpose of worshiping him would have to be the stupidest thing he has ever done. Religion is more tradition than anything else; as there is no scientific evidence whatsoever to support the existence of God, angels or the devil. Still, people cling desperately to the notion of an all-powerful God out there in that mystical place called heaven.

It is fairly clear that some people have allowed themselves to be manipulated, cajoled and literally forced into the belief in God. I understand it of course, because most people live on the edge of a precipice of despair psychologically, emotionally and financially. As

## The Real Jesus Seen in Black and White
## From the Resurrected Spirit of Dixon Frye

my grandfather said, "desperate people cling to religion out of that desperation."

My grandfather said to me, "Wayne, you ever ask yourself why to prove he exists God don't just show up on Walter Cronkite (famous newsman from 1950's, 60's, 70's and 80's)? Or, maybe he should make the sun sit still for a week to show people he exists? Or even better, why not keep anybody from dying for a month? Hey, that would get all the nonbelievers in line."

I once asked my grandfather if he ever prayed. He said, "Yep, I keep praying I admit, but you know what, unlike all them preachers asking for money, God just ain't never had time to talk back to me. Funny how he can talk to all them rich preachers, but never have time to talk to us poor folk."

I asked my grandfather, "What is prayer really, granddaddy?"

"Prayer, now that's a good one. I call it mostly a waste of time. While you busy talking to God about your problem, you could be working at solving it yourself. I think prayer is more about being too scared to tackle the problem yourself. But you know what; I have to admit that scientists done studied prayer. It seems it really can heal people of diseases, but is it the prayer healing them or just plain old will-power. I think

### The Real Jesus Seen in Black and White
### From the Resurrected Spirit of Dixon Frye

unfortunately religion focuses on the evil of humans and teaches followers to be always judging others. The problem here is that this goodness God is supposed to have needs to be used down here not sent up to heaven. After all, there is only happiness in heaven already. Sadness ain't allowed up there with God."

I had been exposed to my grandfather's opinions for many years, and I would often get in trouble at Sunday School, because I would question the teacher about things. I was with my grandparents "down the country" one Sunday, and as usual, my grandmother and her sister went to church, dragging me along, despite my pleading to sleep a little longer. That Sunday, the teacher was talking about how God sent a plague down to kill the first-born all across Egypt in retaliation for the Pharaoh not letting the Jews go. For those unfamiliar with the story, it appears that the Jewish leader Moses, when the Pharaoh had denied Moses' request that his people be freed, said, *"Thus says the Lord: About midnight I will go out through Egypt. Every firstborn in the land of Egypt shall die, from the firstborn of Pharaoh who sits on his throne to the firstborn of the female slave who is behind the hand mill, and all the firstborn of the livestock. Then there will be a loud cry throughout the whole land of Egypt such as has never been or will ever be again. But not a dog shall growl at any of the Israelites - not at people, not at animals - so that*

## The Real Jesus Seen in Black and White
## From the Resurrected Spirit of Dixon Frye

*you may know that the Lord makes a distinction between Egypt and Israel. Then all these officials of yours shall come down to me, and bow low to me, saying, leave us, you and all the people who follow you. After that I will leave.' And in hot anger he left Pharaoh."*

*"At midnight the Lord struck down all the firstborn in the land of Egypt, from the firstborn of Pharaoh who sat on his throne to the firstborn of the prisoner who was in the dungeon, and all the firstborn of the livestock. Pharaoh arose in the night, he and all his officials and all the Egyptians; and there was a loud cry in Egypt, for there was not a house without someone dead. Then he summoned Moses and Aaron in the night, and said, 'Rise up, go away from my people, both you and the Israelites! Go, worship the Lord, as you said. Take your flocks and your herds, as you said, and be gone. And bring a blessing on me too!' So it was done."*

All I did was ask why in the world a loving God would kill so many innocent little children. I postulated that the little babies had not done any of the harm in keeping the Jews in Egypt, so why should they be punished. Even the Pharaoh's son had not kept the Jews in Egypt, as it was his father, so why should he pay for someone else's evil? It didn't seem fair to me. Needless to say, all hell broke lose when I had the nerve to question the teacher. I was thrown out of Sunday

## The Real Jesus Seen in Black and White
## From the Resurrected Spirit of Dixon Frye

School that morning for having the nerve to think. What happened next will require a bit of ancient historical recollection from my own father's past.

As mentioned previously, my grandfather was not a man who suffered fools lightly. When he was told of what had occurred, he looked at my grandmother and said to her, "Vada, I took on a teacher of Worth's long ago for punishing that boy for thinking, and it appears nothing's changed in thirty years. This here boy is using his brain and he done been punished for it. You just don't let some clown abuse your kin folk for thinking. These idiots are scared to death of anybody who has the nerve to think for themselves, I'm gonna have a little talk with that man."

My grandmother was an independent woman, and would stand up to my grandfather when called for, but I could see the fury burning in her eyes, too, because she had been told by a third party that the Sunday School teacher had moved toward the pew where I was sitting and said, "Boy, you are the spawn of the devil." Then he pointed to the back church door and said, "Out you heathen." She simply did not take kindly to her favourite grandchild being called a heathen.

This is where I need to recount a bit of history in regards to my father, and how my grandfather handled a similar incident when my dad was in the sixth grade. For a complete explanation I refer the reader to the biography of my father, where the incident is recorded in great detail, but for our purposes I shall shorten it considerably.

When my dad was in the sixth grade he went to school one day with a condom. Now, remember this was the 1930's, so openness about sexuality was not prevalent in most homes and all schools, as the grip of the church was even more vice-like in those days. His teacher noticed my dad displaying the condom to some other boys and said, "Worth what is that you have in your hand."

Furious, the teacher got up from her desk, went over and held her hand out palm up as she said, "Give that to me. What are you doing with that disgusting thing?"

My dad, a witty person always quick with a quip, replied, "I thought maybe I'd get lucky today."

As the class hysterically laughed, she took him by the hand and went directly to the principal's office. The principal sent him walking the five kilometres home with strict orders to have his mother and father meet with him the next day so an explanation of his impending suspension could be made and his parents could ascertain what punishment they would render along with

## The Real Jesus Seen in Black and White
## From the Resurrected Spirit of Dixon Frye

what was coming from the school. My dejected father showed up frantic with fear, and my grandfather when told what happened said, "We ain't a waiting. Come on, we going to that goddamn principal right now?"

The principal was surprised to see Dixon, as he had expected him the next day. Ushered into his office, Dixon looked around and saw that the motif of the place was austere and intimating. The colour was brown so as to refrain from any indication of frivolity. This was a place of seriousness where no one was expected to ever question the authority of this man who wanted to make sure everyone knew he was in charge. This man was the God of education, or so he thought until meeting up with Dixon Frye.

All my life I have been offended by arrogance, and I suppose that trait is in my genes, as my grandfather that day at school with my father would not bend before arrogance. The principal said, "Mr. Frye, the boy should wait outside."

"No, this is about him. We need to have him in the conversation so he can learn from it."

Somewhat surprised, the principal said, "OK, I will permit it."

"Ain't got nothing to do with you permitting it. That's the way it's gonna be," replied Dixon.

## The Real Jesus Seen in Black and White
## From the Resurrected Spirit of Dixon Frye

The office was bland and austere just like the principal, who started off the conversation by saying that Worth's breach of propriety was a horrible sin. He said, "Anyway, children must learn that any fornication outside of marriage is an abomination. Worth has showed a disregard for probity and scrupulosity that borders on complete disrespect."

The condescending arrogance of the man was on blatant display, as he exuded an air of authority and superiority. Dixon could see that his whole persona was one to induce fear in the children. You do not get respect by using fear. Fear can breed contempt, and, no doubt, thought Dixon, most of the kids probably had contempt for the man. Dixon assumed the man had spent years perfecting his intimidating manner that made kids cower in his presence.

Now, I have talked about control previously as a tenet of religion. Obviously, it can apply to other aspects of life as well, and those with an education are prone to think that they are somehow smarter and better; therefore, should be showed some deference when it comes to respect. My grandfather, my father and my Uncle Lloyd always referred to these arrogant educated people as educated fools. The principal was used to people cowering before him, but he was not dealing with the average person. He was dealing with Dixon Frye. The principal was a man who relished being in control, so he was taken aback when my Grandfather refused to supplicate himself before him.

"Mr. Frye," said the principal, "we have a real problem with a boy bringing a condom to school. The classroom is no place for a condom."

Dixon lowered his head a bit, took a deep breath and said, "First, the classroom is certainly a place for a condom. It shows how intelligent this boy is. He don't intend to get no girl pregnant. If teachers would show boys and girls how to use condoms a lot of heartache could be avoided. As for the big words you keep throwing my way, that don't make you intelligent. You are stupid if you can't communicate with a person."

The principal pointed to the two diplomas hanging on the wall behind him and said, "I have a Master's degree. You don't get that for being dumb."

Dixon said, "That don't prove shit. The world is full of educated fools. Can you even change a tire on an automobile? Can you overhaul an engine on a tractor? Can you replace a carburetor on a car? Can you figure our the right time to plant corn and barley? You know how to slaughter a hog?"

"Of course not. I don't do that kind of work. I am an educator."

### The Real Jesus Seen in Black and White
### From the Resurrected Spirit of Dixon Frye

"Well, you know what; this here boy can do all them things and more, so I'd say he is already smarter than you." Then he pointed at the degrees on the wall and continued. "Them there things on the wall ain't worth shit to you when you out on an old road in the middle of nowhere and your car breaks down. You need somebody with enough sense to fix the car, and chances are the mechanic who can fix it won't have no master's degree. Guess what, this here boy can fix anything on a car. So you know what, I don't think you can teach him anything. He's already smarter than you are." Dixon looked over at my dad and motioned for him to get up. "Come on Worth, they ain't no need for you to come back here, these people can't teach you how to survive in the real world. Hell, they wouldn't last a day in a real job that required some hard work. I got me a master's degree in survival, so I think I can teach you lot more than this fool."

He got up, looked down at the principal and shook his head, turned and walked out the door with my father, leaving the principal sitting there in disbelief.

Now, having recounted the story of how my grandfather was not intimidated by an educated man, it will be easier to understand how he handled me questioning the Sunday School teacher who lived only a short distance from my great aunt's house. As we chortled down the road

## The Real Jesus Seen in Black and White
## From the Resurrected Spirit of Dixon Frye

in his old Chevrolet, I could see a man of great determination and strong will. Dixon Frye was a God to me that day. I looked at his bulky frame, his massive arms, his barrel chest, his thick neck and saw what physical strength looked like, but I saw much more than physical strength. I saw an inner strength that was like a bright light shining in the darkness. He was a man who refused to bend before the winds of adversity, having fought valiantly to get his family through the Great Depression. He had really been on his own since he was eight years old, a boy-man who had to face ridicule, adversity and self-righteous hypocrites pointing the finger of condemnation. He had known poverty's pinch, no poverty's furious bite, but he had been a rock – mighty and strong. Through it all, his iron will was like an anvil – hard, solid and unyielding to any blows from the hammer of discontent. This was a real man!

As a child we are often in reverence of our parents, grandparents, aunts, uncles and older bothers and sisters. It is a feeling that usually diminishes as we get older and see that all individuals, even those we hold in awe, are flawed.

My grandfather was far from a perfect man, but his imperfections paled in comparison to his perfections. He was a man who stood for justice and fairness. He refused to cower before any man, be he exalted or humble. He saw no one as his superior. He refused to be intimidated. His iron will determination made him revered and respected, because he not only stood up for himself, but anyone unjustly put upon by religion or an economic system that crushed people and ground them into service to the moneyed elite. He was a survivor, and he was determined to teach his loved ones how to survive in an unforgiving world.

My grandfather had me in tow as we walked up to the door. He knocked and we waited. He looked down at me and smiled.

The teacher came to the door. He got a stunned look on his face at seeing us, but there was arrogance in his demeanour. He took a deep breath and said, "What can I do for you Dixon?"

"Well, if you a Christian like you claim to be, you'd say, come in. That'd be the polite thing to do. But, based upon your actions today, I ain't so sure you much of a Christian."

"Listen here Dixon, that boy challenged the Lord today. You don't challenge the word of the Lord."

"Well, you may be right, but you see he weren't challenging the Lord was he? He was challenging your interpretation of the Lord's word. There is a big, big difference between the two. This here boy been taught to always ask why. Even if the Lord himself says something, we all got brains and we have a right to ask anybody to tell us why something must be. From what I've read about the Lord, he ain't much for stupidity. He wants people to think and this here boy was thinking which is why he asked the question, and if you don't know the answer, then just say you don't know, and leave it at that, but don't punish someone for having a brain."

"See here Dixon…."

"No, you see here. This boy gonna be in Sunday School ever time we come down here, and he is not an idiot. If 'un you can't defend your words, don't use 'um. I better never see him throwed outta  Sunday School agin for asking a question. End of conversation."

He took me by the hand and we walked away without the teacher saying a word in rebuttal. He just stood there with his jaw hanging down. I crawled into my grandfather's old Chevrolet and looked over at him with great respect as we headed back to my Great Aunt Ethel's house. At the time, I had never heard of what had happened with my father, but years later, when my father would tell me about it, I would realize that the two incidents were very similar, and that Dixon Frye would not stand idly by and allow any of his children or grandchildren to be chastised for the crime of thinking. Today, in retrospect, I realize that Dixon Frye was a mighty man who stood against ignorance and arrogance. He was a man to be reckoned with on the grand stage of life.

LONG AGO, SELECT PEOPLE
CREATED A MONSTER.
IT WAS LET OUT
OF A CAGE BY THESE CREATORS
TO WRECK HAVOC ON MANKIND.
THE CREATORS ARE LONG GONE,
BUT WHAT THEY CREATED STILL
ROAMS THE EARTH
DESTROYING MAN'S
ABILITY TO THINK,
FOR A MAN WHO THINKS IS
A DANGER TO AUTHORITY.
THE ELITES WHO CONTROL THIS
MONSTER SEE TRUTH AS
THEIR ENEMY, FOR TRUTH
SETS PEOPLE FREE.
THIS MONSTER PROMOTES
WAR, BIGOTRY, HATRED AND
JUDGEMENTAL ARROGANCE.
WHAT IS IT? IT IS RELIGION,
AND IT IS NOT THE RELIGION
PREACHED BY THE
MAN FROM GALILEE.

Paraphrase of Dixon Frye's
opinion of religion told to Wayne.

## The Real Jesus Seen in Black and White
## From the Resurrected Spirit of Dixon Frye

*"Every child is born ignorant and that is the way the church wants to keep the child. That is why they want to get little children in Sunday School right away. If they don't get you before your brain develops, then they done lost you."*

..............Dixon Frye on church brainwashing.

## CHAPTER 5
## IMPOSE THEIR WILL UNCONTESTED

*Two prostitutes were riding around town with a sign on top of their car which read, Two Prostitutes - $50.00.*

*A policeman, seeing the sign, stopped them and told them they'd either have to remove the sign or go to jail, because it was illegal under the city by-laws to have a sign on top of a car. Besides, prostitution was illegal.*

*Just at that time, another car passed with a sign that read JESUS SAVES.*

*One of the girls asked the officer, "How come you don't stop them?"*

*"Well, that's a little different," the officer smiled, "You see that is religion, and this is a Christian nation."*

## The Real Jesus Seen in Black and White
## From the Resurrected Spirit of Dixon Frye

*The following day the same police officer noticed the same two hookers driving around with a large sign on top of their car. He figured he had an easy arrest until he read their new sign: Two Fallen Angels Seeking Peter - $50.*

*...........Joke by Dixon Frye overheard by Wayne*

The aforementioned joke was just one way my grandfather had of dealing with the lunacy of self-righteousness and the inordinate cow-towing done by authorities to religion. He would often talk about how he had to pay extra taxes so the church could be tax exempt, the minister even living in a tax exempt home while he had to pay property taxes. He saw the church, as many of the right-wing religious fanatics see welfare recipients – as leeches that drained the government dry. Churches were nothing but giant tax-exempt corporations in his eyes.

I remember my grandfather telling me that many devout Christians had a certain arrogance about them, believing that somehow they were able to control the devil with their praying. They assumed that they served the good of humanity while others were in the realm of evil. He made it plain he felt that they served stupidity because they believed anyone who opposed their doctrine was automatically damned, no questions asked. To him this was the height of arrogance, assuming this self-righteous superiority.

## The Real Jesus Seen in Black and White
## From the Resurrected Spirit of Dixon Frye

One day he said to me when we were discussing religion, "The heaven carrot is dangled in front of Christians by they's religion so they do whatever it takes to get there. So, they ain't doing good cause it's the right thing to do, but cause it is what will get them what they's want – heaven. Or for most it is actually more about avoiding hell, because that is what really scares them. They are just little children frightened by the bogey man."

Looking back on it, though he was not overly articulate, I realize that what he was saying was that religion robbed people of their free will by instilling fear and telling them that their will was irrelevant. They then go out and violate other people's free will as well by preaching their dogma and vilifying those deemed sinners if they don't comply. They believe that anyone who does not obey their God's rules is not worthy and they then practice prejudice and bigotry against these people. They pass judgment in the name of their God on those who do not accept their fear based beliefs.

These people preach disempowerment and ignorance which makes the practice of pure evil possible in the name of God. Evil utilizes the ignorant and fearful for its own ends. Today, I marvel at so many of my old high school classmates who wanted to befriend me on Facebook, and probably regret it now. They are

## The Real Jesus Seen in Black and White
## From the Resurrected Spirit of Dixon Frye

old and perhaps I should be more tolerant, but I am appalled at how they are still trapped in the past, still fighting the Cold War, still believe that prayer in schools will somehow cure all the ills of America, that keeping guns in the hands of all will somehow quill the terrorists who want to destroy the American way of life. They are clinging to "old time religion" like it is a panacea for all the ills of a world that has simply passed them by. They do not have the ability to deal with a world where religion is questioned.

Sin is attached to Christians like a ball and chain and they cannot escape it or change direction until they are kicking up daisies. They are oppressed, but they are so brainwashed they actually line up for their ball and chains.

These Christians are constantly told of their sinful nature by ministers who often do exactly what they tell the congregation is evil. Christians spend their lives believing they are tarnished. Their religion is based on three things - fear, lies, and obedience. Fear is the basis of all negative emotions which they are told to avoid. Their God on the other hand has no qualms whatsoever about expressing these negative emotions through his frequent acts of wrath and mass murder. He therefore sets a very bad example by his actions. It is imperative that the church leaders utilize fear to keep the money rolling in and the people in constant consternation.

J. Wayne Frye

## The Real Jesus Seen in Black and White
## From the Resurrected Spirit of Dixon Frye

These people obey without realizing that they are enslaving themselves. Ignorance is blissfulness for these people. They refuse to seek out any counter argument to their beliefs. They fear knowledge, because they are taught that the only knowledge worthwhile is in the Bible. These are the same people who ridicule Muslims for strict adherence the Koran.

It is very similar to people who will only watch FOX NEWS, because it substantiates their preconceived notions. My grandfather never categorically stated that he did not believe in Jesus. He just voiced his doubts of Biblical truth. He believed in self-reliance and knowledge. He once told me, "It is noble to teach people to love one another, but we also have to take care of ourselves, because God just aint' gonna do it. Ask God to put food on your table and see what happens. I don't think God ever fed my children. I got out and worked to do it. If 'un there was a Jesus, from what I read, he tried to teach people to think for themselves and care for each other but religion twisted his words around to say that we have to always rely on God to do it. Hey, my youngins' and wife and me wuda gone hungry in the depression if 'un we depended on God for food. Mark my word good and remember it well. They is one person in this world you have to depend on, and it ain't no God up in the sky. It is you. Family may try to help, but they ain't always around. In the end, it's just you."

## The Real Jesus Seen in Black and White
## From the Resurrected Spirit of Dixon Frye

God's will is always an anomaly to me, as is how people are always attributing things to it. I recall the time I saw on television many years ago a man who got the licence plate number of a pedophile who had killed a six year old girl. He boldly claimed, "God put me there to get the licence number of that evil beast." Where was God when the little girl was being molested and killed? Seems to me like God was a bit derelict in his duty as our protector to allow the little girl to be raped and killed.

This is the kind of lunacy that used to drive my grandfather crazy. He believed that people were just simple minded, like children. He believed that if humans did not start thinking for themselves and throw off the doctrine and dogma of religion that the world simply could not evolve. The idea of a jealous, angry and vengeful God he saw as a ploy to keep us in submission and stagnation. Strangely enough, according to religion, ignorance is not a sin, because blind belief without question is the height of reverence for God. Christians are supposed to suspend independent thought and blindly believe.

Once my Grandfather, in my words, not his, said in effect, "Christ may have claimed to be God but he almost certainly meant that he was a part of God as are equally the rest of us. In Psalms 82:6 and John 10:34, God and Christ actually say "Ye are gods," yet Christians continue to turn a blind eye to this interesting piece of information. In fact the plural gods appears numerous times in the Bible which might lead an intelligent Christian to question the proclamation that there is only one God in all of creation.

The fact that Christianity has been practicing deception is incredibly obvious. The creation story in Genesis is a simplistic fairy tale that any five year old would laugh at if told by some adult. Yet, adults gobble it up.

Religion is a structure which feeds the people pabulum fairy tales to keep itself going financially as well as maintaining its power. Its greatest fear is knowledge. Muslims want to march backward to the 12th century, but Christians do not offer much better, because they all long for a past when religion exerted more control over America and the world. The truth is that the American Christians who decry the Taliban and ISIS would love to exercise that type control over the American people. These are the people who support water-boarding and torture in the name of righteousness. If they love Jesus so much how could they not demand that the USA honour his admonitions against torture, cruelty, worship of money and the promulgation of war?

Where were the clergy while Bush and Cheney escaped prosecution for their war crimes?

## The Real Jesus Seen in Black and White
## From the Resurrected Spirit of Dixon Frye

If it wasn't for the people's ignorance and desires to give away their personal power to authority, the entire clergy would be out of a job and would have to start working for a living. One only has to apply a little critical thinking to what religion puts forward to see the deception and subtle immoralities. Practical solutions to problems are ignored, and everything is turned over to God. This is the same God that has allowed abomination after abomination for all time. Righteousness is not bestowed by some God. It is bestowed by one's actions toward other human beings.

I once ask my grandfather what one had to do in order to go to heaven. He smiled and said, "Well my guess is three things: Number one is accept Jesus as your savoir, number two is be obedient – very obedient as your church says, and number three, and the most important one, keep filling up the collection plate. Basically, you get to heaven by being dumb and not challenging authority. Funny how we are told God's love is unconditional, but then all kinds of conditions are put on it. We are expected to do what the church says, because we ain't smart enough to think for ourselves."

Now, it has been so long ago that I do not remember what I thought at the time, but looking back I believe that even in my young mind I would have thought that religion seeks to divert

## The Real Jesus Seen in Black and White
## From the Resurrected Spirit of Dixon Frye

our attention away from our inner self and focus it onto an invisible and inconceivable ruler of our lives and that the church is like any other ruler as its aim is self-perpetuation and control. Rejecting religion's doctrine of God does not result in hell and blindly believing in God does not result in heaven. Many here on earth are already in hell for a variety of reasons. On the other hand, people like my grandfather who refused to be a slave to religion were, in a sense, already in heaven, because they were free of the hell imposed by ignorance and blind obedience to religion.

Love is complete acceptance and respect for another's freedom and choices while always being ready to help as much as possible. My grandfather was revered and admired for his intense commitment to giving a hand up to the downtrodden. That is why when he died, more people turned out for his funeral than any other in the history of Asheboro, North Carolina. He did not need religion to guide him to righteousness or his salvation.

We all must make profound choices in life. In my own life, since about 1964, I have been guided by the spirit of Che Guevara, a man whom I believe my grandfather would have admired. Che once said, "I could have been a doctor in an affluent suburb of Buenos Aires, and maybe helped two or three thousand people in my

## The Real Jesus Seen in Black and White
## From the Resurrected Spirit of Dixon Frye

lifetime who were all born into affluence, or I could turn my back on all that affluence and become a revolutionary and help millions of people who struggle to put food on their tables every day."

Unfortunately, I am no Che Guevara as I have neither the bravery nor commitment he had, but I do try to always be on the side of the downtrodden, and like my dear grandfather, extend the hand of compassion.

When I was in the U.S. Army during Vietnam, I saw first hand what my grandfather taught me about hypocrisy. He always said that the government liked to tell people how free they were, but, in reality, the government was scared to give the people too much freedom, because if they had too much freedom those in charge would be overthrown by irate citizens who would figure out they were not so free after all. In Vietnam, the USA feared the communist takeover, because the communists wanted to utilize an equalitarian system of governance that would not allow elites to control the economy. The war actually had nothing to do with defending freedom, and being privy to top secret information, I began to see exactly what my grandfather meant. The American government represents a cabal of the wealthy elite who want to control world finance so that they and their families benefit at the expense of the common man.

## The Real Jesus Seen in Black and White
## From the Resurrected Spirit of Dixon Frye

My grandfather instinctively understood this, and maybe didn't even realize what he understood, but he saw religion and the U.S. government working hand-in-hand to keep people in chains. As long as the poor think they will get their reward in the by and by, they will not put too much demand on government in the here and now. In the process, the government must always keep people afraid, and during the Cold War, government used the simple mindedness of the religious people to manipulate them into fear that the communists were lurking about ready to take away freedom and their right to worship God.

In reality, the communists eliminated the power of the church and replaced it with the power of the state. The truth is there were never any real pure communist nations, only pretenders to communism, as like the USA and its vaunted democracy that is a farce, communist nations in the Cold War with the exception of Tito's Yugoslavia, Castro's Cuba, Ho's North Vietnam and Mao's China were only caricatures of communism used by dictators to maintain power. Americans, as my grandfather saw them, were too stupid to realize they lived in a dictatorship that was disguised as a democracy. This was the way my grandfather saw it, although he was not articulate enough to put it in the descriptive words I used here. He once told me with great conviction, "them there communists are the best thing ever happened to the rich people in America, cause they can use them to keep the poor people afraid and everybody scared that they gonna lose the right to let the church run their lives. We always being told 'bout how communists is brainwashing people, but what does the church do? I don't see no difference, brainwashing is brainwashing no matter who does it."

I spent part of my time during the war at the Pentagon, and it was there that I learned to truly respect the astute observations my grandfather made when I was a youth. I was an intelligence analyst with the Joint Chiefs of Staff, and the chicanery I saw was appalling and opened my eyes to the realization that the idea of America always being righteous was a gigantic lie. The underhandedness, lying, manipulating and constant violation of international law was commonplace. My grandfather had told me that in World War I the people were told that they were defending freedom, and then the government promptly locked up anyone who spoke out against the war, accusing them of treason. This was the height of hypocrisy, but that is America. The World War I Sedition Act was almost as onerous as the Patriot Act. World War II saw interment camps set up to house the Japanese-Americans, not as bad as the reservation system for Native Americans or the concentration camps in Europe, but they were a

## The Real Jesus Seen in Black and White
## From the Resurrected Spirit of Dixon Frye

deplorable example of what happened when you dare stand against the U.S. government, and during Vietnam, demonstrators were mercilessly slaughtered by a government that simply could not tolerate dissent. When Iraq came along the dynamic had changed as the draft had been eliminated so the rich and privileged did not have to die in senseless wars. If the children of the rich had to go to those places and die for "freedom" there would have been more outrage, but using the poor for cannon fodder is a time honoured American tradition now, and ironically, the poor actually line up to defend the freedom they don't even have. They cannot understand that real freedom is only reserved for the elite.

My service during the Vietnam War was after my grandfather's death, but that service made so much of what he taught me crystal clear. I began to see things in a more critical light as the years of patriotic brainwashing flowed into a river of reality. The churches actually encouraged that war, except for a few brave ministers who defied convention and stood against the tyranny, and years later, when Bush and Cheney lied the nation into another immoral and illegal war, the churches did nothing to expose the folly of the ill-advised adventure. While the poor died so Bush could prove his manhood to his father, his children were safe in university and the children and grandchildren of the members of Congress did not have to dodge bullets.

## The Real Jesus Seen in Black and White
## From the Resurrected Spirit of Dixon Frye

Dixon Frye never realized his influence on me, and I never realized it either until much later in life, but his steady hand and words of wisdom have made me a better person, a person who questions authority and never bows to the tyranny of the elite class that wants to rule with impunity and impose their will uncontested.

**The Real Jesus Seen in Black and White**
**From the Resurrected Spirit of Dixon Frye**

## CHAPTER 6
## CHOKE US ON THEIR HYPOCRISY

*The devil is dancing on the steps*
*Smiling with glorious glee.*
*He looks up and laughs as hypocrites*
*Parade through the golden doors.*
*How they prance about in finery,*
*Displaying arrogance and vanity.*
*Ah, they do not realize they worship*
*Not the Prince of Peace in this place*
*For their hypocrisy slaps Jesus in his face.*

*They bow before the dark one,*
*Who tells them greed is good.*
*They believe the lies of false prophets*
*Who in pompadoured hair*
*And thousand dollar suits spout evil*
*That is an affront to the man from Galilee.*
*This is an abomination of all that is holy.*
*Jesus sheds a tear up on high*
*And lets out a forlorn sigh.*

J. Wayne Frye

## The Real Jesus Seen in Black and White
## From the Resurrected Spirit of Dixon Frye

*AND THUS IS THE DOOR OF HYPOCRISY*
*OPENED FOR DIXON TO SEE AND HEAR*
*AS BUTLERISMS PREVAIL AGAINST FEAR*
*IN CADENCE TO ROCK AND DANCE*
*THE FOUNDATIONS OF ARROGANCE*

*Sir Arrogant his passing worth,*
*The stiff manner how he sallied forth;*
*His arms and equipage are shown;*
*His fancy virtues are all his own.*
*The adventure of the guitar and fiddle*
*Is sung, but breaks off in the middle.*

*When civil fury first grew high,*
*And men fell out, they knew not why;*
*When hard words, jealousies, and fears,*
*Set folks together by the ears,*
*And made them fight, like mad or drunk,*
*For damn religion, as for punk;*
*Whose honesty they all doth swear for,*
*Though not one of them knew wherefore.*

*When Gospel-Trumpeter, surrounded*
*With long-eared rout, to battle sounded,*
*And pulpit, drum ecclesiastic,*
*Was beat with fist, and a carrot stick;*
*Then did Sir Arrogance abandon dwelling,*
*And out he rode about colonelling.*
*A dandy he was, whose very sight would*
*Make those people bow before he stood.*
*He never bent his stubborn knee*
*For he carried Jesus for all to see.*

J. Wayne Frye

**The Real Jesus Seen in Black and White**
**From the Resurrected Spirit of Dixon Frye**

*He could deliver with tongue a righteous blow.*
*This is what the people wanted to know*
*As they turned soul over to deceiver*
*Who was so pompous and arrogant.*
*Either for cartel or for warrant;*
*Great in the fiery pulpit of despair,*
*He sat on a hypocrite's golden saddle,*
*And he would prance and swaddle.*

*Mighty he was at all these,*
*And styled he war, as if it was peace.*
*Outweighed his rage was full grain;*
*Which made some take him for a tool.*
*The knave he was playing for a fool,*
*As deceit for him was the golden rule.*
*Far too few saw him for an ass,*
*As most let his lies simply pass.*

*He had grand and glorious wit,*
*And was not shy about using it;*
*As being loath to wear it out,*
*He bandied it all about,*
*As if he was the holy one*
*When all was said and done.*
*Ah, but pigs do so horribly squeak.*
*And he climbed arrogance's peak.*

*Getting rich was easy with deceit*
*For the sheep were blind to defeat.*
*His bounty came from those who wanted*
*Jesus all honoured and exalted.*
*This salvation most could not afford*

## The Real Jesus Seen in Black and White
## From the Resurrected Spirit of Dixon Frye

*This buying their way to the Lord.*
*He told them to give until it hurts,*
*Cause Jesus must get his just deserts.*

*Now Dixon Frye sat before T.V.*
*And the deceit he could see.*
*"This charlatan," he told grandson*
*Is seeking riches and fame.*
*He could say a man is a horse,*
*Vow hypocrisy is a great force,*
*Say the sky is not blue but pink*
*And into the mindless it would sink."*

*No one dare this hypocrite to dispute,*
*For he is a minister beyond rebuke.*
*He'd undertake to prove, by force*
*The argument, a man is a horse;*
*He'd prove a buzzard is a fowl,*
*And that man should hoot like an owl.*
*His rhetoric was far, far beyond disputation,*
*For he represented the Lord of grand reputation.*

*He ranted and raved against sin,*
*While he himself sat in the devil's den.*
*With great artfulness he spoke,*
*Appealing to the poor mindless folk.*
*For all a rhetorician's glorious rules,*
*He thought he had control of fools.*
*His speech had the cadence of disdain,*
*As he listed from what all must refrain.*

*Teach nothing but to judge and condemn:*

J. Wayne Frye

## The Real Jesus Seen in Black and White
## From the Resurrected Spirit of Dixon Frye

*He danced on abomination's rim.*
*Dixon sat and shook his head at the gabble*
*And thought it was gibberish babble.*
*For the minister would coin, or counterfeit*
*New words, with great ponderous wit:*
*Words so debased and hard, no stone*
*Was hard enough to touch them on.*

*With grand voice he filled their cup.*
*Ah, the ignorant gobbled them up.*
*The sheep hung on his every phrase.*
*They were enamoured with his ways.*
*Dixon said, "He cons on a great scale,*
*And the fearful gobble up his ale."*
*Dixon shook his head in disgust,*
*As all compassionate men must.*

*"Study this man well grandson,*
*For when all is said and done,*
*He teaches marketing like a pro.*
*His techniques lay sanity low."*
*Dixon eased back in his chair*
*For of people like this he had no fear.*
*But he was smarter than most in the land*
*Where Christians had heads buried in sand.*

*Watching Billy Graham and Oral Roberts on TV,*
*He thought a reasonable person could easily see*
*This Jesus thing was nothing but a money machine*
*Hatched in a room with greed hungry and lean.*
*These people praised Jesus so well,*
*But the truth they would never really tell.*

J. Wayne Frye

## The Real Jesus Seen in Black and White
## From the Resurrected Spirit of Dixon Frye

*They could reduce all things to Godly acts*
*As if life itself was not filled with abstracts.*
*They fed pabulum to adults who were children,*
*While stirring up discontent in an evil cauldron.*

*Dixon laughed out loud at what some said,*
*Especially about Gabriel's horn raising the dead.*
*"What a mess," he told his grandson,*
*"But at least the dead would have some fun.*
*They'd kick their coffin lids off in glee,*
*Then rise out of the ground all happy."*
*Together we laughed in voices high,*
*As he said, "And elephants can fly."*

*Sir Arrogant was on TV and radio a lot,*
*Hatching his sinister money plot.*
*He could raise scruples dark and nice,*
*And after solve them in a trice;*
*As if Divinity had been his catch*
*And the lord the soul would scratch.*
*Just give and give with a little pain,*
*And eternity is what you will gain.*
*Oh, what the sinner can find,*
*When on the lord he decides to dine.*
*There is a seat reserved in paradise,*
*So with your money do not be concise.*

*Below the moon, or else above it,*
*Adam dreamed of bliss when his bride*
*Came from the rib in his side:*
*But the old devil tempted her*
*As evil's great interpreter.*

J. Wayne Frye

## The Real Jesus Seen in Black and White
## From the Resurrected Spirit of Dixon Frye

*It was the wily serpent that made Eve fall.*
*Now says Mr. Arrogant payment is made by all.*
*So, let that paper money float into the plate,*
*And you shall be rescued from an evil fate.*
*Mr. Arrogant's religion was so fit,*
*Because he manipulated with wit.*
*Presbyterian, Catholic, Baptist all could be blue.*
*Methodist, Seven Days could join them too.*
*You see only Mr. Arrogant had Jesus' address,*
*And it took money to right your sinful mess.*

*He ranted against Christians being put upon,*
*Encouraged the faithful not to surrender gun.*
*Controversy can be solved by faith and artillery,*
*As in gun-crazy America it is Jesus' distillery.*
*He declared only the righteous are the intended,*
*As wavering from the path can never be defended.*
*Free-will all the faithful must one way disavow,*
*Disharmony simply Mr. Arrogant cannot allow.*

*All piety consists with him therein,*
*Only he can interpret each and every sin.*
*Do not ever defy or question this man of God*
*For he transverses holy, sanctified sod.*
*His saintliness you must never oppose,*
*As he makes the pig sty palpable to the nose.*
*Hypocrisy and nonsense be too dumb to see*
*And just keep tossing in eternity's holy fee.*

*Yes, Dixon saw Mr. Arrogant time and again*
*In the pulpit preaching against mortal sin,*
*But he had his number in his jack-ass stall.*

J. Wayne Frye          91

## The Real Jesus Seen in Black and White
## From the Resurrected Spirit of Dixon Frye

*That is why Old Dixon never gave him a call!*

Television in those days was not in colour and grandfather used to say, "TV preachers are perfect for black and white, because that is the way they see everything. They see no shades of grey, no bright colours at all. They only promise you darkness if you sin. People are like children. They fear darkness. But, when these fancy talking snake oil salesmen get colour, watch out! They will use red to scare people of the fiery hell that will consume them if 'un they don't give Jesus his due, and what is Jesus' due – your money, of course. The favourite colour for these carnival barkers, for the church, is green, the green of U.S. dollars, but one dollar bills won't get you into heaven as fast as 20 dollar bills, and a 100 dollar bill will make old Saint Peter smile from ear to ear."

"Look around you boy at these preachers fancy cars, their palace-like homes, their fine clothes, the diamond rings sparkling on their fingers, and go into their churches that would make a king green with envy. These people preach and preach about helping your fellow man, and they keep the church doors locked to keep out the riff-raff. They says send in your money to help the poor, but all you helping is the church or preacher to get rich. They go down to some ghetto and act like they helping people. Let me tell you a story about how much they help people. I done figured out that who they helping the most is they-selves."

## The Real Jesus Seen in Black and White
## From the Resurrected Spirit of Dixon Frye

This was a day that my education in scepticism was fed a healthy dose of Dixon Frye situational observations on hypocrisy. It is something that I have observed time and time again over the years, and I am thankful each time for the knowledge handed me by such a wise man. As we sat again on that swing where he shared so many witticisms of grand and glorious enlightenment, he said, "Boy, you wanna hear a good story?"

As usual, I replied, "Sure granddaddy," as I adjusted my position and got ready.

During the war I remember seeing old boxing champion Jack Dempsey on posters telling Americans boys to sign up to fight Hitler. Now listen here, Hitler was an evil man and we outta fought him, but you don't lie people into joining up to fight. I remember the first time I ever seen that sign. I looked right down at old Jack standing there among the crowd in Hell's Kitchen in New York, just like he was one of them poor people, one of the crowd. Only trouble was he had on overhauls and an old shirt, but you looked down at his shoes and he forgot to take off his $100 loafers. One thing about rich people, even the ones that got outta being poor, they can't let go of that stuff they thinks makes 'um somebody. Now that there preacher Billy Graham, he lives up in Montreat on a fancy estate. He keeps telling us how God loves the poor, how we need to turn our backs on riches and find the things that count.

## The Real Jesus Seen in Black and White
## From the Resurrected Spirit of Dixon Frye

Seems kind of like a hypocrite to me, living like that while preachin' agin piling up all them material things. Ever seen them high priced suits he wears? Just don't seem right to me preachin' one thing and doin' another."

"Then there's that darn Oral Roberts. Now how he pulls off all that healing he does is somethin' else, though my guess is he's somehow got it all rigged up, or them people just so stupid they actually believe all his baloney and heal themselves for a few minutes, but my guess is them cancers they has comes back after awhile. Gotta give that boy credit though, he don't dress fancy like them other ones does. He rolls his sleeves up and acts like a country boy, and I been to one of his tent meetings. He gets right down among the people and mingles with 'um. He rants and raves, prances and dances, shouts and hollers. Yep, that boy can put on a real good show. I put a quarter in his collection plate cause it was better then going to the movies. He is a better salesmen than them fancy preachers is. He goes after the real poor folks cause they much easier marks. He done found his treasure ain't in the high-toned places but down amongst the poor who need Jesus a lot more than them rich folks."

I could not resist asking, "Don't they ever get caught for stealing people's money granddaddy? I mean isn't it illegal to do what they are doing? They are stealing aren't they?"

## The Real Jesus Seen in Black and White
## From the Resurrected Spirit of Dixon Frye

"Of course theys stealing boy, but they stealing for the Lord, and that is the problem, so nobody wants to prove it. Government, all them politicians is afeared of getting people upset. Them politicians know these guys can deliver poor folks' votes, get them poor to vote against their own best interests. You just don't go up agin' Jesus." Then he winked at me, because he knew I was old enough to know about sex, as he continued, "That'll get you voted out quicker than being caught with a two dollar whore."

We enjoyed a grand laugh together as he continued his tirade against the evils perpetrated by religion. "You know what? How'd people ever come to worship a God that done so many cruel, nasty, evil things to people? Why in the Old Testament he encourages you to murder your own children. Like I said to you before, he done slew the first born children in Egypt because of his hatred for the Pharaoh. What's those innocent kids ever do to God? Now people are always working on Sundays today. I even go out and work on my car or truck on Sundays, but God done told his followers to kill everybody that works on Sunday. So, the poor man who has to work Sundays to feed his family is supposed to be put to death according to God. What's this God want from his followers? You follow most of his rules but you break just one and he has himself a darned hissy-fit like you wouldn't believe and decides to send down hail-stones to kill you and your children. Now, even if your children don't work on Sunday, he commands they be killed right along with you."

I rarely interrupted him when he was in one of his rambling proclamations of disdain for religion, but I could not resist. "Yeah granddaddy, what is it with all these things he does to people who disobey him. I mean aren't we all entitled to a few mistakes in life?"

"Go figure boy. Go figure why he told his followers to arm themselves with swords and slay every man, his brother, his companion and his neighbour in God's name. Now, that is a lot of killing for God, and I done thought he was supposed to love us all. And what about forgiving people? Didn't Jesus say we was supposed to forgive? I mean if 'un we did what God said in the Old Testament they'd be no time for much else but killing. He even said kill adulterers. Now that one alone would net millions of deaths for sure. Why when people used to displease him, according to the Bible, he'd send plagues to destroy them. Why he even told a crowd to kill a man who gathered sticks on the Sabbath for violating his commandment. He done told his followers to kill every male child of captured women, then kill the women, but keep the young girls for themselves to enjoy. Yeah, that is a real loving God alright. None of that stuff makes any sense, but people is so desperate for meaning to they's lives, they blindly follow this nasty God."

## The Real Jesus Seen in Black and White
## From the Resurrected Spirit of Dixon Frye

That porch and that swing were the place where I learned valuable life lessons, and above all, learned to think for myself, courtesy of a man who had taught his children the same ideals. My aunt, my uncle and my father were all independent thinkers courtesy of the wise sage named Dixon Frye. On this Sunday, I was about to truly learn that this was a man of great wisdom from a time when most people were scared to stand against the tyranny of religion. He never cowered before the pontificators of hate. He saw through the fantasy of fanciful farces perpetrated on the poor, unthinking masses that lived in the darkness and thought it was the light.

He sighed deeply, and said, "You know I ain't sure there ever was a Jesus, but some of the things they say he did and said makes lots of sense. If 'un he was real, he sure had no use for hypocrites, which they's plenty of in the church today. Now you know what a Pharisee is right boy?"

"Sure," I confidently replied, "They were the opinionated and self-glorifying group of leaders in Jerusalem. They were like lots of people today who believe in miracles, resurrection, angels and spirits. Things like that. But they were arrogant and loved to display their superiority because of their beliefs. They looked down on sinners and promoted themselves as righteous, yet their religion was all about outward show. They were all show but no substance."

## The Real Jesus Seen in Black and White
## From the Resurrected Spirit of Dixon Frye

"Well put boy. You better with words than me. You gonna be an educated boy one day I bet. But always remember they's lots of smart people who ain't educated, mostly cause they are poor and never got the chance to be educated, and this here world is ruled by those who want to keep people ignorant, cause ignorant people don't question authority."

"I know that granddaddy, because I have an uneducated grandfather, father and uncle who are about the smartest people I will ever know."

He laughed and said, "You got that right, son." He then eased back in the swing, looked out into the darkness and said, "You may have heard this story before, but it's good to repeat some stories 'cause they are lessons in what really counts in life. Remember that whether there is a God or not don't really matter. We all here on this earth for a short while and what we need to do is help each other as much as we can, 'cause one thing for sure, the rich ain't never gonna help us poor folk, and the government ain't gonna help nobody but the rich. We gotta learn to judge people by what's in the heart not they's bank account. If 'un there was a man named Jesus, he knew that, and he made it plain that what counts is a heart full of love, mercy, humility and goodness. These was the kind of qualities the Pharisees didn't have way back then and modern Pharisees don't got none of that either."

## The Real Jesus Seen in Black and White
## From the Resurrected Spirit of Dixon Frye

"Now Jesus was asked by a Pharisee to eat with him and he went into the Pharisee's house and ate at the table. And a woman of the city, who was a bad sinner, found out that he was in the Pharisee's house. She brought some ointment, and standing beeside Jesus at his feet, weeping, she began to wet his feet with her tears and wiped them with the hair of her head. She kissed his feet and anointed them with the ointment. Well, when the Pharisee who had invited him saw this, he said to himself, 'If this man were a prophet, he would know what sort of woman is touching him, for she is a sinner.' And Jesus knew what he was thinking. Jesus said, 'Simon, there was a moneylender who had two debtors. One owed him five hundred denarii, and the other fifty. When they could not pay, he cancelled the debt of both. Now Simon, which of them will love him more?' Simon answered, 'I suppose the one for whom he cancelled the larger debt.' Jesus said to him, 'You have judged rightly.' Then turning toward the woman Jesus said to Simon, 'Do you see this woman? I entered your house and you gave me no water for my feet, but she has wet my feet with her tears and wiped them with her hair. You gave me no kiss, but from the time I came in she has not stopped kissing my feet. You did not anoint my head with oil, but she has anointed my feet with ointment. So I tell you Simon, her sins, though many, are forgiven, for she loved much. But he who is forgiven little, loves little.' And Jesus said to the woman, 'Your sins are forgiven.' Then those

who were at table with him began to say among
themselves, 'Who is this, who even forgives
sins?' And Jesus said to the woman, 'Your faith
has saved you; go in peace.' You see boy, we all
sinners one way or another. Ain't nobody perfect,
and in my mind that even includes Jesus, cause
even he had a doubt for a few seconds when he
was on that cross and said, 'Father why hath thou
forsaken me?' This here parable tells you that you
have to realize that sins and doubts will always
crop up in our lives."

I smiled and said, "But you aren't through are
you granddaddy?"

He smiled back and said, "Simon the Pharisee
has a problem with the way a woman sinner is
treating Jesus and his acceptance of her. She was
kissing his feet, wiping them with her hair and her
tears, and she was anointing them with perfume.
Simon could not see the loveliness of this act. He
could see only the sins she had committed, and he
could only despise her. As for the two men who
owed money, both were forgiven their debts by a
compassionate moneylender. The moneylender in
this parable represents God, and the two
debtors represent sinners. You see, God in the
New Testament is made kinder by his son Jesus,
just like I am made kinder cause of my love for
my grandson. When Simon was asked to choose
which of the debtors he thought would love the
moneylender more, the answer was very simple as

it would be the one who owed the most. So God is saying that the sinner woman is more worthy of his love than the Pharisee who sees himself as righteous. Jesus was hard on Simon, but perfectly fair. Simon had shown no love for Jesus, and even fell short of courtesy. The woman, the sinner, had shown great love and faith. Hey, the church is full of Pharisees today who love to condemn but do not know how to embrace and show forgiveness. I ain't perfect son, and I can carry me a grudge as well as the next man, but if 'un you fair with me and show that you ain't judging me nor looking down your nose at me cause I don't think like you do or cause I am poor, you alright, but I be gall-darned if 'un I'll ever put up with arrogance from anybody, and that includes the Queen of England and the President of this here country."

I sat in awe just staring at him as he continued. "Now I ain't got much use for government tax collectors cause they always coming after us poor folks for taxes while they let corporations and the wealthy with their fancy, high-priced lawyers get away with not paying much taxes, but Jesus done figured out in one tale that even tax collectors are human, and they got families to support. They's work might not be what I'd call a very good way to make a living, but I understand we all gotta put food on our tables. Jesus was always agin' hypocrites which is what I like about him. He once told a parable to some who trusted in themselves that they was righteous, and could judge others."

## The Real Jesus Seen in Black and White
## From the Resurrected Spirit of Dixon Frye

Here was a man with no use for religion or the Bible, but his knowledge of the Bible rivalled any theologian's. His eyes lit up with delight as he continued. "Two men went up into the temple to pray. One was a Pharisee and the other a tax collector. The Pharisee stood praying to himself, 'God, I thank you that I am not like other men, extortionists, unjust, adulterers, or even like this tax collector. I fast twice a week; I give tithes of all I get.' But the tax collector, standing well back, would not even lift up his eyes to heaven, but beat his breast, saying, 'God, be merciful to me, a sinner!' Now, Jesus said that the tax collector was better than the Pharisee. For in heaven Jesus said that everyone who exalts himself will be humbled, but the one who humbles himself will be exalted. Jesus you sees, just had absolutely no use for hypocrites as he said they are like whitewashed tombs, which outwardly appear beautiful, but within are full of dead people's bones and all is filthy. So he saw the Pharisees as outwardly appearing righteous to others, but within full of hypocrisy. Jesus had no use for people who were so public about praying. I mean he would not even want prayers said by self-serving politicians in public, because he saw these people for what they are – hypocrites. That is the real Jesus, Wayne. He'd look at all these television preachers and shake his head in disbelief that anyone could be stupid enough to fall for the malarkey they dish out from their mouths like it was coming straight from Jesus hisself."

J. Wayne Frye

## The Real Jesus Seen in Black and White
## From the Resurrected Spirit of Dixon Frye

My grandfather was a fan of *Huckleberry Finn*. It was probably one of the few books, other than the Bible, that he read in his entire life. Every so often a piece of literature is written that can question the beliefs of millions of people with what they hold to be true. Nothing is held to be truer than the feeling of righteousness, being faithful, morally pure, and the idea of an exalted higher purpose through religion. *The Adventures of Huckleberry Finn* questions this. Indirectly, Mark Twain argues and criticizes the religious hypocrisy of the American culture. Through the brilliant use of satire and anecdote, the author conveys his repulsion of hypocrisy practiced by so-called Christians. As a runaway boy, Huck Finn has the painstaking choice of doing the right thing, according to Christianity of the time, by writing a letter to the owner of a runaway slave who is with him and tell where the slave is, or go to hell if he helps the slave named Jim, his friend. Christian morality was ballyhooed by a church that condoned slavery and it taught Huck to give Jim to his owner, but Huck sacrifices himself to a higher morality than that offered by a hypocritical church. Defying his religious teachings, ironically, Huck does the most Christ like thing. This was pointed out to me often by my grandfather, who, himself, had difficulty with prejudice against Blacks, as he was a product of a south that had made first slavery and then the draconian Jim Crow laws part of a culture that kept Blacks in their place – an inferior place as defined by God.

## The Real Jesus Seen in Black and White
## From the Resurrected Spirit of Dixon Frye

Twain would have had a field day with the Islamophobia of today, as in the book he shows how the Christian church felt about people from different countries and religions, while preaching tolerance. One incident of hypocrisy my grandfather liked to point out from the book was the incident when Tom Sawyer persists for Jim to play a Jew's Harp to attract rats, and the snakes, and spiders. The reader can see the inference that the Christian church preaches that snakes, rats and spiders which represent the devil will engulf anyone who tries to play the Jew's harp. In other words, Jews are evil, because they do not accept Christ. They are put in the same category as rats, snakes and spiders.

My mother was from a family of religious fanatics who were mostly members of the World Wide Church of God. Many times I heard their ministers lay the blame for Christ's crucifixion at the feet of the Jews, who when given a choice by Pontius Pilot of which prisoner to release, chose the rebel, Barabbas. So, thousands of years later, living Jews were expected to pay for the sins of their forefathers. This kind of convoluted thinking is what drove my grandfather into a rage against religious hypocrisy.

One of his favourite lines to me was, "Wayne, if 'un them Christians had their way, they'd shove Jesus down all our throats and choke us on their hypocrisy."

J. Wayne Frye

**The Real Jesus Seen in Black and White**
**From the Resurrected Spirit of Dixon Frye**

## CHAPTER 7
## AT THE FEET OF A GIANT

*So God gave some a licence to steal.*
*The preachers are picking your pockets clean,*
*While making sure you answer their appeal.*
*An hour with them and your finances are lean.*

*They see the sheep ready for the fleece.*
*They'll tell you the Lord is your friend,*
*And they got Jesus for you on a long term lease.*
*Give money and he will forget you sinned.*

*Church is where the poor go and come out poorer.*
*Church is not about salvation but collections.*
*Squeezing from the poor you can't sink lower,*
*Telling people to pay for Jesus' affections.*

*Preachers do all this in the name of the Lord.*
*They know all the verses about giving,*
*And how the sinners suffer the righteous sword.*
*You stay poor while they enjoy high living.*

J. Wayne Frye                105

## The Real Jesus Seen in Black and White
## From the Resurrected Spirit of Dixon Frye

Not all ministers are thieves, neither are all thieves ministers, though it appears the two are highly compatible. The world, almost from the beginning of time has been hit by a Tsunami of spiritual degradation. The church has been transformed from a spiritual haven to a business empire. With tax free offerings a guarantee, every thief probably longs for the huge plunder of those who proclaim themselves servants of God. Dixon Frye saw this hypocrisy long ago, and this was a life-long obsession with him – how religion was used to make its preachers wealthy.

Dixon looked at his sons, Worth and Lloyd, as they were working furiously on two cars in the garage behind his house. Dixon walked over, looked down at the engine in one and said, "Pretty nice job of souping up the engine, but if 'un all you doing is driving back and forth to the store don't see why you need so much power. Don't see no numbers on the cars, so you boys must not be planning on racing 'um. Just from the looks, I'd bet if I raised that damn trunk lid, I'd find me a great big two hundred gallon tank in it for carrying moonshine." He scratched his bald head, walked to the entrance, looked back over his left shoulder and said, "If 'un you boys planning on running shine, keep in mind your mamma would be a mighty hurt woman if anything happened to you two. Worth, Lloyd here is your baby brother, you 'spose to look after him. You better see that you do."

## The Real Jesus Seen in Black and White
## From the Resurrected Spirit of Dixon Frye

Dixon Frye had a very disarming way of letting you know he was no fool. Truth is that Worth and Lloyd were planning on running moonshine, but that little talk made Worth see to it that the under age Lloyd only worked on the cars and didn't do any transporting. Dixon knew that poor boys had very little opportunity in a country run by and for the elite. Most of the poor who became successful had to skirt the law in order to do it. Dixon was a realist, and the reason he stopped at three children was because he knew that you didn't bring children you couldn't afford into the world. The country was full of over-producing poor people encouraged by the church to be fruitful and multiply. However, that multiplying was just providing workers for the rich to take advantage of in their factories. "Goddamn church," he used to say, "they want 'um born, but they don't do a damn thing to help 'um after they born. Pop 'um out, put 'um to work and tell them Jesus loves a cheerful giver so they'll put 10% of their meagre earnings in the collection plate."

Dixon saw things differently than most people, as he was more perceptive than those who fell for the manipulative manifestations of patriotic flag-waving that made people believe they had to defend liberty, when what they had was not liberty at all but a mere propagandized glorification of something that did not exist for the average working person. Patriotism was a game played by the powerful to get the poor to die for causes that a perceptive person could see were simply diversions to keep people in fear of some outside entity that wanted to destroy the American way of life. The truth was what people had to fear the most was their own government that was bought and paid for by the wealthy and the corporations.

I may be a bit more eloquent than he was in describing the way he felt about patriotism, but the gist of it is simply that he could see though the manipulative nature of patriotism and applied the same perceptive analysis to the church which used the same techniques to trap people into a prison of their own minds. Whether it was church or patriotism, the key was to get the young children and indoctrinate them before they developed the power to think for themselves. This was a man with a grade three education but the analytical mind of a person with a Ph.D.

Now running moonshine was a very common way for young men to accumulate some money and go into legitimate businesses. Dixon saw no harm when he supplied the bootleggers with sugar during prohibition from 1921 until 1933. He said, "Them damn 'publicans give the Bible-thumpers what they wanted, but you gotta be damn stupid if 'un you think you gonna keep people from drinkin'. Mark my words, them Bible-thumpers is going as the saying goes reap what they sow. They done sowed a wind, and they gonna reap the whirlwind. Lawlessness will rule this land."

## The Real Jesus Seen in Black and White
## From the Resurrected Spirit of Dixon Frye

Moon-shining has been a strong tradition in the Southern Appalachian mountains for hundreds of years. It was a prime source of income for generations of mountain people. Historically, it was one of the few ways to earn cash in the subsistence-dominated mountain economy. It is the basis for many local stories and an important part of the mountain myth of individualism and resistance to outside authority. It has thrived in spite of legal and religious condemnation. Though today it is a rarity, the legend of the moonshiners lives on. One of those legends is my father, Worth Frye, who one night while on one of his northern runs, tore up the town of Chillicothe, Ohio in a wild chase with the local police. Of course, that is a subject of another book, so I shall not detail it here. Suffice it to say, that it is a fading tradition since the late 1950's when the price of sugar soared. While it is disappearing from the local scene, its legacy is still felt. Moonshine was a strong but secretive presence in mountain counties. This secrecy is evident in local peoples' drinking habits. I never saw my own father ever take a mixed drink. He drank it mountain style, straight, followed by a chaser. He always said, if you gonna drink, you should drink, and that damn sissy drinking mixed drinks is for them city boys not us southerners. I would not know, because I never took a drink in my life. However, like my grandfather, I figure drinking and doing drugs is your own business, and like religion, if you don't force it on me, go right ahead and enjoy yourself.

## The Real Jesus Seen in Black and White
## From the Resurrected Spirit of Dixon Frye

Prohibition was a boon for southerners who had a little still and could run off a gallon or two. It spawned a whole new cottage industry as people were even making gin in their bathtubs. The giant spirits corporations actually were tossed under the bus by the usual protectors of corporate interests, the Republicans. Having been out of power for eight years, they made a bargain with religion to bring in prohibition if votes could be delivered, and votes were indeed delivered. So, prohibition was introduced and America became a "dry land." However, while the federal government was busting up stills and jailing bootleggers, they simply could not keep up with the number of stills that were popping up. While they were shutting one down, two more would start operating, so lucrative was the business. The same mentality that thought up the war on drugs created the idea for prohibition. You will never defeat drugs and you will never defeat man's desire for alcohol. My grandfather always said, "Find a vice, and a way to satisfy it and you can get rich. I never drunk a drop of liquor nor ever done no drugs, but I ain't gonna stand in the way of any man wants to do either. I made myself a pretty good living for a long time supplying bootleggers with sugar, and I ain't ashamed of it. People gonna drink and ain't no damn government or no damn religion gonna keep 'um from doing it. You think you gonna stop it, you just a dang fool. People drink cause they's lives is miserable. And that misery is caused by a being poor,  and government ain't never gonna do

**The Real Jesus Seen in Black and White**
**From the Resurrected Spirit of Dixon Frye**

a damn thing about that neither, cause they too busy taking care of the wealthy to worry about the poor."

My grandmother and grandfather used to tell me stories of how people hid their "mixins" from the authorities. Some used to hide it in false bottoms of pickle barrels, down dry wells and others hid it under the bassinets where a baby would be sleeping. Usually, the shiners would have their stills far back in the hills safe from prying eyes. My grandmother loved to play her autoharp and sing a song that was written during the depression about a moonshiner.

*There's a big hollow tree*
*down the road here from me*
*Where you lay down a dollar or two*
*You stroll 'round the bend*
*and you'll come back again*

*There's a jug full of good old mountain dew*
*They call it that mountain dew*
*And them that refuse it are few*
*I'll hush up my mug if you fill up my jug*
*With that good old mountain dew*

*My uncle Mort, he's sawed off and short*
*He measures about four foot two*
*But he thinks he's a giant*
*when you give him a pint*
*Of that good old mountain dew*

J. Wayne Frye                    111

## The Real Jesus Seen in Black and White
## From the Resurrected Spirit of Dixon Frye

*Well, my old aunt June*
*bought some brand new perfume*
*It had such a sweet smelling pew*
*But to her surprise when she had it analyzed*
*It was nothing but good old mountain dew*

*Well, my brother Bill's got a still on the hill*
*Where he runs off a gallon or two*
*The buzzards in the sky*
*get so drunk they can't fly*
*From smelling that good old mountain dew*

*There's a jug full of good old mountain dew*
*They call it that mountain dew*
*And them that refuse it are few*
*I'll hush up my mug if you fill up my jug*
*With that good old mountain dew*

Dixon was a man who was not very tolerant of religion, because of the hypocrisy he saw displayed, but he was always willing to give a man his due when he saw the light of compassion in him. His neighbour was a car dealer named Bud Essick, and Bud was a man with a big heart and a predilection toward accepting people without pointing the finger of condemnation. Much younger than Dixon, Bud would often come by to sit and talk with him. As they sit on the porch one night, I remember Bud saying, "Dixon, I got a little problem. There's a man stealing from me, but I know why he is doing it. He just don't make enough, and he's got some big hospital bills."

## The Real Jesus Seen in Black and White
## From the Resurrected Spirit of Dixon Frye

"Well Bud, I know who you talking about and his hospital bills is for his little boy who is dying of leukemia, right?"

"Yes, the boy doesn't have long I think."

Now I was listening intently, as I fiddled unnoticed behind the porch with a rain barrel, but I knew who he was talking about too, because I had played with the boy a few times when his family had visited Bud."

Long before even Canada had free healthcare, my grandfather was way ahead of his time, because he understood the unfairness of a system that punished people for getting ill. I did not realize it at the time, but that night on the porch, my grandfather showed an intense comprehension of the inherent evil in for-profit healthcare. "Bud, stealing from a man ain't right, but you know what, making people who is poor die cause they can't pay ain't right either. I hear tale that them folks in Europe is doing the right thing and making healthcare free for everybody. This here country ain't never gonna do that cause it is too selfish, too worried about profits to ever do the right thing by folks. The damn church oughtta be demanding that poor people get healthcare just like the rich does. But they more worried about who somebody's sleeping with than they are about some child dying cause his daddy ain't got the money to pay."

## The Real Jesus Seen in Black and White
## From the Resurrected Spirit of Dixon Frye

He eased back in the swing, and I noticed he glanced over his shoulder, because he knew I was listening. He said, "Sorry 'bout the cussing Bud. Truth is I doubt he stole much from you."

Nodding his head affirmatively, Bud said, "Not much, just about one hundred dollars."

"How long he worked for you Bud?"

"Six years."

"He been a good loyal employee all that time?"

"He has, yes."

"Hey, what he done ain't right, but he's got plenty of trouble right now. My guess is he's probably done an extra hundred dollars worth of work for you in all those years. I know he's a good mechanic, so he has made a lot of customers happy. Forget the money. It ain't that much, and you know what, you can afford it. This damn country is pretty bad when it drives a man to steal just to see his boy gets proper medical care."

"You're right Dixon. I'll forget it. I know you forgot a lot of debts from people in trouble over the years."

Granddaddy nodded in the positive and went back to swinging, as he said, "Get up here boy."

## The Real Jesus Seen in Black and White
## From the Resurrected Spirit of Dixon Frye

I joined him and Bud. A week later Bud was on vacation with his family and they had a horrible automobile accident and Bud was killed. In all these years, this is the first time I have ever revealed this story. Ironically, the man's son died a few weeks after Bud's death, and the man, when the car dealership closed, went to work for my father, and I never said anything to my father about the incident. Within a few weeks of his employment with my dad, my grandfather also died from a massive heart attack. Many years later, I was talking to Bud's wife, and she mentioned how much her husband valued my grandfather's friendship and advice. She said, "You know what Wayne, your daddy once came by to see me a long time ago, and he brought Danny Denweiler with him. It was about something you know about. You see, Bud told me about a conversation he had with your granddaddy about a week before he was killed. Bud said you were playing behind the porch and overheard the conversation they had about Danny."

I was a young man home for vacation from university at the time, and I said, "Yes Eunice. I remember the conversation well, but I never told anyone about it."

"Well, I just thought you should know that Danny came by with your dad, and Danny paid me the hundred dollars he stole all those years ago. I just thought you should know."

## The Real Jesus Seen in Black and White
## From the Resurrected Spirit of Dixon Frye

Since I was friends with Danny's living son, I was thrilled to know that the debt had been settled after all those years.

Eunice had one more thing to say as I turned to leave. "Wayne, your granddaddy was the finest man I ever knew. When Bud was killed, I know your granddaddy never told anybody, but he came down to see me about a month after it happened, and he knew that Bud didn't leave us that well-off, but he told me, "Eunice, you ever need anything, just let me know. I'll do the best I can to help you. Your granddaddy was a big, burly man who could be tough, but he had the softest heart of any man I ever knew."

I smiled, said not a word, but walked away with my shoulders held back and my chest puffed out. I took a deep breath and sighed as I got into my car. I wiped a tear from my right eye and thought to myself that I had once sat at the feet of a giant of a man.

**The Real Jesus Seen in Black and White**
**From the Resurrected Spirit of Dixon Frye**

## CHAPTER 8
## NO SANITY WITH RELIGION

*With your mouth you speak falsities,*
*From your lips pour empty praise,*
*Of honour you have absolutely none,*
*You call to God to bless your days,*
*You publicly declare you love him,*
*In vanity you worship him,*
*And you mock others in sermons,*
*For your heart is trapped in deceit.*

*Take away all your fancy words,*
*Your religious mockery,*
*For you show only shallowness.*
*Your heart is far from the exalted one.*
*Strip away self-righteous gowns,*
*End all your vain expressions,*
*Take your laws and throw them down,*
*Cease your false confessions of piousness.*

*Clanging harangues against sin*

## The Real Jesus Seen in Black and White
## From the Resurrected Spirit of Dixon Frye

*Are echoes from a hollow shell.*
*Your skill makes people tremble,*
*But there is a God who knows you well.*
*With your lips you shout his praises*
*But in your heart you only have deceit.*
*Your false honour is despicable,*
*Praising saintliness while practicing devilry.*

*I bend not before your hallow deception.*
*I see you for the charlatan you are.*
*My, oh my, how the flock is mesmerized,*
*As they can not see you are evil's Czar.*
*You use religion like a shining star,*
*But it lights not the darkness that abounds*
*In your manipulative monstrous soul.*
*You are the ill wind of dark evil.*
*Oh, you are the true and real devil.*

*.....Paraphrased poem once recited by Dixon Frye*

As we age, we see things in better perspective. I actually always loved my grandmother more than my grandfather, and frankly, still do. However, as time has passed, I realize that much of the good in me is a result of a grandfather whom I often looked on with distaste for his grumpiness. That goodness is also attributable to my Aunt Willa Mae, Uncle Lloyd and my father, because their outlook on life was based on a foundation laid by Dixon Frye and my sainted grandmother. We all, for good and bad, are profoundly affected by the environment in which we were reared.

J. Wayne Frye

## The Real Jesus Seen in Black and White
## From the Resurrected Spirit of Dixon Frye

Today, I realize that a man whom I often looked upon with dislike was really a profound influence on me and those he loved, those he called friends, and even those whom he might have designated enemies. Just looking at an editorial cartoon that I designed, an article I wrote or even things that someone else might have contributed makes me reflect on how my grandfather influenced my thoughts and perceptions on life or how his ideals are reflected in what others think, feel and say. Though uneducated and inarticulate, I now, more than ever before, see the depth of his wisdom. I always sensed his love, despite his often harsh manner, and later in life, I saw his lack of ability to utter the simple words "I love you" as a contributory factor in my own father's feelings of being unloved by him. How strange is it that we too often commit the sins of the father. My own father had trouble with those words, "I love you." On the other hand, my father's and grandfather's lack of the ability to utter those words made me never tire of telling my own three children "I love you."

The Frye side of my family was not known for religious virtuosity, at least not my grandfather, grandmother, father and mother; though my cousins are, I assume, fairly religious up to a point, as they attend church with some regularity. Still, my own outlook on religion is more reflective of my father, grandfather and mother. I see, as they did, religion as more of a harbinger of

## The Real Jesus Seen in Black and White
## From the Resurrected Spirit of Dixon Frye

evil than good, based upon its hypocrisy and utter reliance on what Dixon Frye and now me, see as a belief in fairy tales. I put aside fairly tales when I was a child, and until I see an angel hovering over my head, an absolute unimpeachable miracle by that ever elusive God who has plans for our lives, an unequivocally solid piece of evidence that the Jews were ever even in Egypt, an irrefutable artefact showing Jesus ever walked the earth, or the spirit of the Savoir manifests itself on the sofa across from Jerry Fallon, I shall continue to entertain my serious doubts. Now, if there is a Jesus, the Jesus I would want to worship would not show disdain for a doubter, but admiration for using a brain that the ever elusive God I always hear about gave me to use not let atrophy.

As mentioned, there is not much I embrace politically and religiously that is not a reflection of what I was taught by Dixon Frye and his son Worth. Let me share a few examples of what I believe is an accurate reflection of what Dixon Frye taught me in regards to religion as he saw it. Sometimes images can be better than words, but when you can combine words and images, you often have an even more profound effect. I have been a published writer since I was 15 and submitted my first editorial to the *Greensboro Daily News*. An editorial to which I signed a pseudonym for fear the politically conservative and narrow-minded Christians in my hometown might take offence. Now, frankly, I don't give, as my grandfather would have dismissively said, " a good goddamn whom I offend." There simply are some great prerogatives that go with age. The difference between me and my grandfather is it took age to make me fearless with my thoughts. For him, it was natural from birth.

*This is a perfect illustration of how my grandfather would have viewed the hypocrisy practiced by Christians over gay marriage.*

I never once heard him make a derogatory comment  about being gay; although at the time, the term used would have been "queer" by the typical southerner. He did once tell me when we were talking about a man who was arrested for making a pass at a man in a restaurant. "Well, they says he's a queer, but why should that get you arrested. If you ain't interested, all you gotta say is

## The Real Jesus Seen in Black and White
## From the Resurrected Spirit of Dixon Frye

"no thanks."

Even in his long ago day, he saw the utter lunacy of the church's obsession with homosexuality and it complete lack of finding truth, which is the subject illustrated by the below that appeared in publications across the world.

**WHEN TRUTH COMES**
**BY**
**J. Wayne Frye**
When truth comes,
the landscape listens.
Shadows hold their breath
in anticipation.
When truth lights
the night with brightness,
injustice is rectified
and sanctity prevails.
There is no truth
like the truth of love.

Truth is an elusive commodity in a world where politicians repeat lie after lie to accommodate

## The Real Jesus Seen in Black and White
## From the Resurrected Spirit of Dixon Frye

those from whom they seek votes, and churches promulgate half-truths and distortions to manipulate and control the sheep that blindly follow them to slaughter. Truth is not what most people want. They prefer to live a lie in order to convince themselves that there is something waiting for them after this life. They are so bewildered and confused that they simply want someone else to do their thinking for them.

My grandfather understood better than most how people were too simple minded and too easily manipulated to see the veil of deceit that was used to keep them in chains. Thinking actually takes effort, so it is easier to let someone else do it for you. Those of us old enough, for example, can remember quality television with symphonies, operas, plays, ballet, etc. that stimulated the mind, but today's television is nothing but ridiculous carnival-like sideshows displaying the stupidity of Americans. It is almost as if being stupid is to be celebrated. I can remember a time when singers did not have to have outlandish clothing, parade around nearly naked, utilized flashing lights, coloured haze and other special effects to attract attention. The purpose of all the aforementioned is not to provide quality entertainment, but hide the lack of talent being displayed by those who are participating willingly in the dumbing-down of America to satisfy their greed. For those of us old enough to remember quality television and entertainment, it is a big disappointment, but to younger people, they have already been brainwashed into accepting mediocrity. In a fit of discontent over rising cable bills that provided me with 450 channels, but made me realize that 450 channels of junk is still junk, in 2009, I got rid of mediocre television, and my life has improved immeasurably as a result. I am a better conversationalist, a more voracious reader and have produced three times as many books each year. If I want entertainment, I can get on You-tube and watch old television shows from the 1950's and 1960's or quality black and white films from the 1930's and 1940's without profanity, blatant nudity, simulated sex and outlandish special effects, because they actually have a story to tell that might require some brain power.

Truth was something you always received from my grandfather, as he was a man who simply told you like it is. I often tell people that I am an equal opportunity offender. In a sense, my grandfather taught me that, because he always said, "If you tell people the truth, it'll piss 'um off, and I have sure pissed a lot of people off in my life."

Now, like him, I try to never, under any circumstances, tell the truth in a hurtful way, as he also said, "Wayne, you can tell people they are stupid without calling them stupid." Yet, I think, although I never heard him do it even once in my presence, that he might have called my father stupid, and my father was one of the smartest men

**The Real Jesus Seen in Black and White**
**From the Resurrected Spirit of Dixon Frye**

I ever knew. My own father was always calling me stupid, and it is a word I judiciously avoided with my children. I can think of nothing more hurtful than being told by a parent that you are stupid, especially when, like me, you really are pretty stupid. My oldest son asked me once in regards to my accumulation of assets, "How did you do it dad?" I said, "Ken, I did it by being frugal, because I was smart enough to know I wasn't smart."

Now, when it came to healthcare, as mentioned previously, my grandfather was a man of compassion. He was far ahead of his time in believing it was a human right, and would have certainly believed that Jesus would have supported it as such. In fact, he often asked why the church could sit idly by and allow such an abominable system that was anathema to everything Jesus stood for.

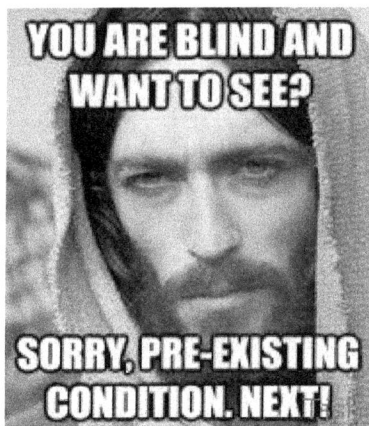

YOU ARE BLIND AND WANT TO SEE?

SORRY, PRE-EXISTING CONDITION. NEXT!

## The Real Jesus Seen in Black and White
## From the Resurrected Spirit of Dixon Frye

The appalling nature of American for-profit healthcare was not lost on him even before its abject insidiousness became as apparent as it is today. He saw, even in the 1950's, the inherent evilness of a system that would only treat you if you had the money to pay. He would often say, "I don't know which is worse, the people who run the hospitals and will let you die on their steps if you can't pay or that damnable church that talks about the love of Jesus and allows this to go on. A good preacher would be leading his flock down to the hospital and say to that person running it that God would send a plague of destruction on this place if 'un you don't change. No, they'd rather talk about you going to hell for some sin. How about the sin of greed that'll let a child or old person die cause they can't pay? Now that is the kind of sin Jesus would be upset about."

As one can clearly deduce, Dixon Frye had no use for Republicans, as he saw them as I do – the party of the wealthy and corporations. He, like me, found it ironic that the poor would so often vote Republican, and thereby vote against their self-interest. He told me once, "Just can't figure people out who think the 'publicans is gonna do anything for the poor. They's been agin' everything that ever helped the poor. Why old people drawing their social security vote for 'publicans without even giving thought to the fact they's the very people who fought it tooth and nail – called it socialism to let old people have enough to eat."

## The Real Jesus Seen in Black and White
## From the Resurrected Spirit of Dixon Frye

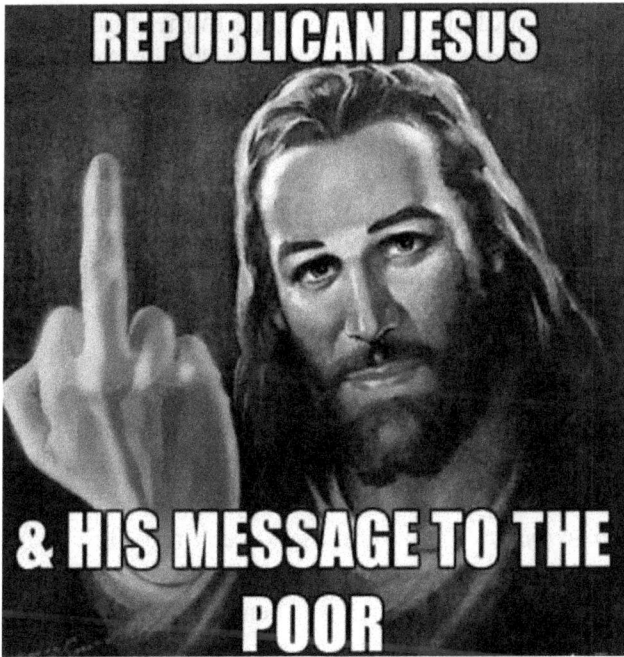

REPUBLICAN JESUS & HIS MESSAGE TO THE POOR

My grandfather rarely used profanity in front of me, but one day a minister was at Clyde Steed's Texaco Gas Station while I was having some of my beloved Buttercup ice cream with my grandfather. An election was on the horizon, and he was encouraging the people there to vote Republican, as he said they were the party more attuned with the works of Jesus. My grandfather, sat in an old cane back chair listening to everyone agree that the Republicans would keep the Christian tradition alive and well in America and make sure those new-fangled, commie beatniks didn't destroy the country.

J. Wayne Frye

### The Real Jesus Seen in Black and White
### From the Resurrected Spirit of Dixon Frye

My grandfather had only gone to the third grade, but he knew the Bible and he knew American history, which meant he was thoroughly attuned to the separation of church and state. He looked at the preacher, and for effect, he used profanity to let him know exactly what he thought of him and his love for Republicans. "I tell you what preacher. I don't think you know a goddamn thing about the Jesus I done read about. You say the 'publicans represent what Jesus wants. Frankly, I don't think you'd know Jesus if he showed up at this here gas station and bit you on the ass. One thing for sure, you'd point your finger at him and call him one of those goddamn beatniks (*forerunners of hippies*). Let me tell you something about the Jesus I learned about. I think Jesus was one of those beatniks you running down. He had long hair, wore sandals like them and dressed like a damn bum. He didn't hang out with the rich folks either. He hung out with crooks, prostitutes and lepers. You'd run from all three and say the devil was in 'um. He was anti-death penalty, anti-public prayer and anti-wealthy – read your goddamn Bible, if you can't remember the book and verses, let me know cause I know 'um all. He was no white man either, so you need to open up your church to the coloureds. And if I was you, I'd keep my mouth shut about telling people how to vote. They's laws in this here country says churches ain't supposed to politic." He got out of his chair, motioned for me to get in the car and said, "Let's go boy."

## The Real Jesus Seen in Black and White
## From the Resurrected Spirit of Dixon Frye

As he took my hand he said, "Yep, lets go home." Then he looked at his friends and said, "You fellows can sit here and listen to his bullshit if you want to. I got better things to do."

I sat in the front seat of the Chevrolet proud that I was with a man who was unafraid of anything, especially pontificating ministers of mayhem who spread their vile hatred like an ancient plague among the unsuspecting masses. Dixon Frye was like my hero on television, superman. He was a man of steel!

On the way back home I asked him about ancient plagues and why they were worse than they were now. He laughed and said, "Because God sent them down, and he can really work up a good plague."

For some reason, my question led to a philosophical musing from him. He said, "You know what boy? They's all kinds of plagues. Some ain't diseases like we normally know 'um. I mean they's a plague going on in this country right now. People are afraid. Fear spreads like a plague and them 'publicans and even some Democrats love to make people afraid, afraid of some country that ain't like ours. I mean Russia is the best thing ever happened to the 'publican party, cause people is scared of them Russians. Scared they'll take away our freedom, so the 'publicans play on that fear."

## The Real Jesus Seen in Black and White
## From the Resurrected Spirit of Dixon Frye

"What you mean play on fear, granddaddy?"

"They use people's fears to get them all riled up, get them in a frenzy. Scared people is easy to control. People afraid can't be reasoned with. It is just like that preacher. He thinks he is right cause God is on his side. Now, that is a plague too – religion. It spreads all over the world and causes all kinds of mischief cause people think God's on they's side and the other side is the devil. You can't compromise with them people cause like I said, they thinks God's on they's side, so they can't be wrong."

Today, in a world where the radical Muslims are blowing people up and radical Christians believe torture is acceptable when used against the aforementioned Muslims, I often reflect on my grandfather's wise assessment of religion, and how it is used to manipulate and control people. The Old Testament is alive and well in a world where an eye for an eye and a tooth for a tooth trumps sanity. In fact, as my grandfather would probably have said, "They ain't no sanity when it comes to religion."

**The Real Jesus Seen in Black and White**
**From the Resurrected Spirit of Dixon Frye**

## CHAPTER 9
## AIN'T NOTHING THERE

*Hey, this dude was a one man revolution*
*He was actually very scary,*
*taking up the cross he had to carry.*
*The truth about him would make you leery.*
*He was a grass roots communist activist*
*before Malcolm and Marcus arrived.*

*At the age of 12 he was ready to rock and roll,*
*tackling scholars in the temple with his soul.*
*Jesus was a damn revolutionary.*
*This dude was a grand visionary*
*whose rousing words are legendary.*
*But he was actually very contrary.*

*He supposedly gave sight to the blind,*
*had the power to raise the dead,*
*fed the masses that were hungry*
*with a few fish and several loaves of bread.*
*Pharisees questioned one so young,*

## The Real Jesus Seen in Black and White
## From the Resurrected Spirit of Dixon Frye

*but this dude wasn't done.*

*He said very clear and very loud,*
*as he roused the crowd:*
*"I didn't come to bring peace,*
*I gotta sword to unleash."*
*"Do not bow before tyranny," he said.*
*So the powerful wanted him dead.*

*Jesus was a revolutionary divine.*
*This dude turned water into wine;*
*told his disciples at the last supper*
*that he was about to end his time,*
*but not to worry because revolution*
*would one day make the sun shine.*

*He showed man how to be truly free.*
*But the preachers of the word can't see.*
*They are blinded with a myopic view*
*that just won't give this man his due.*
*The mindless cannot understand the reactionary.*
*Dude, accept it. Jesus was a revolutionary.*

Dixon Frye was a man who learned that in America you were on your own, because the government was owned lock, stock and barrel by the wealthy and corporations. His life was not easy as a child, because of the stigma attached to being born out of wedlock, but he never bowed before the tyranny of the religious paragons of virtue who were always ready to point the finger of condemnation.

J. Wayne Frye

## The Real Jesus Seen in Black and White
## From the Resurrected Spirit of Dixon Frye

Maybe it was this arrogant self-righteousness and finger pointing that soured him on religion at an early age. Still, I believe he would have questioned religion regardless, simply because he was too intelligent to not give serious thought to the lunacy of believing things that simply were beyond the realm of possibility. He used to laugh at the absurdity of many Bible tales. One of his favourites was the preposterousness of Noah and the flood. He would shake his head and say, "Do these idiots really believe that a man got one of every animal on earth on a boat that was smaller than the Titanic? These people need to have brain surgery and see if 'un they can't maybe get some doctor to put some brains in they's empty heads."

Most people read the Bible and don't realize that what they are reading has been edited and reedited over the years. However, Dixon Frye had read many different Bibles, and despite his meagre education, he had searched out that which the typical Christian does not even have any idea exists. His favourite left-out stories were shared with me on many occasions, and I shall not detail them all here, but perhaps what follows is a good example of how he never accepted what he was told by ministers as the definitive tales of Jesus. He knew that the church did not want everything about Jesus revealed, but only that which supported the contentions made by the church. Too much truth is not good for the mindless sheep who need to be manipulated and controlled.

**The Real Jesus Seen in Black and White**
**From the Resurrected Spirit of Dixon Frye**

As was often the case, one evening we were sitting in the swing and my grandmother was reading her Bible in the fading light of day. Dixon said, "Vada, you gonna ruin your eyes reading in the dark. Anyway, that book is a bunch of gobble-di-gook. Why don't I tell you and Wayne a story that ain't in that book but should be. A story about Jesus that the church don't want told."

My grandmother smiled and said, "Does it make any difference whether I want to hear it or not?"

"Not really, I'm gonna tell it anyway."

Thus, he began his tale of how the church allowed a pagan holiday to become the celebration of Jesus' birth. "You think Jesus was born on December 25 like most people who just accept everything they told by the preachers. Now, it don't make no difference to me when he was born, 'cause I got my doubts he ever was born, but I done studied about Israel in them cyclopaedias your grandmother wasted money on."

My grandmother couldn't resist, she interrupted and said, "Yea, we don't need no encyclopaedias when we got Dixon Frye."

He ignored her comment and continued. "In the town of Bethlehem, they's a church built over the place where they say Jesus was born. November through early March is winter in Israel! The weather gets cold, especially at night. Often it rains or even snows! Most people are shocked at how cold it is there. I mean this is supposed to be a hot country. Now, first of all, I ain't convinced that there was ever a manger there. I'd guess it might all be some smart business people started this whole thing as a way to get Christians to flock there and spend money."

"Now, if these Christians is smart, they'd take a look at the weather and realize something. In Luke it says, "There were in the same country shepherds abiding in the field, keeping watch over their flock by night. People who know anything know that this could never have occurred in Judea in the month of December. In them times and even today, they brought their flocks in October at the latest. So, it weren't December, couldn't have been. So, Jesus simply weren't born in December. Now, you got a grandfather what knows the Bible. Mary became pregnant with Jesus when her cousin Elizabeth was six months pregnant with a child who would later be known as John the Baptist. Jesus, then, would have been born six months after John. If we could know the time of John's birth, we could then simply add six months and know the time of Jesus' birth. John, according to the Bible, with a little smart arithmetic was born in late March or early April. Six months after that, Jesus would have been born, in late September or early October, before the sheep was brought in from the fields."

## The Real Jesus Seen in Black and White
## From the Resurrected Spirit of Dixon Frye

You could sense that my grandfather was enjoying showing how astute he was at figuring things out. He continued. "Late September or early October was also the time of year that taxes were paid, in the fall, at the end of the harvest. Joseph and Mary, remember was going to Bethlehem to be taxed. The fact that there was no room for them in the inn also tells the time of the autumn harvest, because the annual fall festivals occurring at that time attracted many Jews to Jerusalem and nearby towns, filling all the rooms. So, like so many other things with religion, this December birth thing is all lies. Just didn't happen. Now, if the church can lie about that, how many other things does it lie about?"

My grandmother, shaking her head, said, "And now you gonna tell him that this whole thing was cooked up by merchants to sell presents."

Not cracking a smile, Dixon said, "Don't have to. You already just told him." Still, he could not resist adding something else. "If God had wanted us to observe Christ's birthday, I think he'd given us the exact date and instructions on how to observe it, but he didn't! Christmas is an invention of the church and a bunch of smart businessmen who figure that it is a good way you get people to part with their hard earned money. Wouldn't be the first time the church ever hooked up with business. Hey, what you think the church is but a giant tax-dodging corporation anyway."

**The Real Jesus Seen in Black and White**
**From the Resurrected Spirit of Dixon Frye**

Dixon Frye was a quiet man who was able to let his words flow effortlessly to make a point. Though he would be considered extremely inarticulate with the words he used, still the way he used them was sometimes spellbinding for their directness. He was not shy, just a man who kept his words to a minimum and was direct, but sometimes he would get wound up. This was one of those nights when he would display his knowledge of the Bible. The truth was the man had basically memorized the entire Bible, as he often kept the most skilled purveyors of the word mesmerized with his ability to quote chapter and verse almost verbatim.

"Yep boy, Christmas is not about Jesus. They pretend it is, but the truth is that it is about people making money. The money changers Jesus threw out of the temple are back and they are making more money than ever. They are basically dancing on his grave. They all right back the way they always was. The church is full on the holidays and that collection plate is over flowing. Look at ever thing the church does, every thing this country does and it always has a dollar sign attached. That fool Herbert Hoover said during the depression that the corporations had to be protected from failure cause they were vital to America. That tells you right from the get-go that the 'publicans ain't concerned about the poor man or the man in between. All they care about is the moneyed class and they'll do anything to protect they's interests."

## The Real Jesus Seen in Black and White
## From the Resurrected Spirit of Dixon Frye

"Look at the church, and you'll see that the big moneyed boys get to sit down front so they can be seen. So they can show off how successful they are. Look at the way peoples dress on a Sunday – puts on their finery to show off, to prance about like peacocks. Yep, Jesus threw them out, but they's back in full force."

I was curious. "Granddaddy, sometimes I have trouble understanding about hypocrisy."

"Let me tell you a story boy. Maybe that will help."

He eased back in the swing and got that confident air about him the way he always did when he knew he was about to deliver a blow against hypocrisy. "Have you ever woke up from a nightmare, only to find the terror stayed with you after the dream was over? You remember your disappointment and concern when you found out the Tooth Fairy is really a parent? Often, as we age, we begin to question things like why do parents lie about Santa Claus? I mean isn't it hypocritical to tell your children not to lie and then you lie to them about things like that? Well, let me tell you a story about a fella and how things all changed for him in the flick of an eye. Yep, there are times when you least expect it that something comes outta the clear blue, outta nowhere and afterword nothing is ever the same agin."

## The Real Jesus Seen in Black and White
## From the Resurrected Spirit of Dixon Frye

"Yes granddaddy, I remember when I found out about the tooth fairy. That was when I started doubting about Santa Claus too. I did ask myself at that time why adults would lie to me about that, and maybe if they lied to me about that they were lying about other things too."

"Ah, yes, that in itself is a form of hypocrisy. Telling children not to lie and then you do it. Now, the same applies to religion. How many people really belief the tomfoolery that is in the Bible. I mean come on, but we send children to Sunday School and let them be told all those whoppers. Let me tell you a story Wayne."

"Sure granddaddy. Go ahead."

"First, there are permissible lies. I mean if a person asks you how they looks, I mean you wouldn't want to say to them that they look like a fat cow. So, we do have to be polite in life, or at least we should be. Now, we already know that parents lies to they's kids all the time. Santa Claus, the tooth fairy and the Easter bunny are good examples. Think about all the times before they invented the printin' press, which wasn't that long ago, and they had people copying from old Bibles. Now, you don't have to be no scholar to figure out that maybe the church didn't like the way things was said, so they just had the copiers change a little here and there. Then the next copiers changed a little more and on and on."

## The Real Jesus Seen in Black and White
## From the Resurrected Spirit of Dixon Frye

"Yes, I see granddaddy. So, you are saying the Bible could have been altered over all these years?"

"Yep, don't see why not, boy. The world is full of people who lie for their own benefit. If 'un people believe certain things about God and Jesus, why that might give the church more control over people's lives. And you know what? Most people actually want to be controlled, cause they too stupid to think for they-selves. Never seen many people in church challenge the preacher or the Sunday School teacher like you done. And you remember what happened when you did. The church just don't want nobody questioning it, cause God knows best. Well, God may know best, but I ain't never seen no sign that the church is God, or for that matter even God-like if 'un you give it serious thought. Jesus sure never woulda sit foot in most of the churches I been in."

"So, you saying the church has lied?"

"Ain't saying no such thing, but am saying it is possible, and in my book highly likely. Now, be honest boy, ain't you lied a time or two to keep from gettin punished or to get what you want outta somebody."

I shamefully nodded my head affirmatively and said, "Hate to admit it granddaddy, but yes I have."

## The Real Jesus Seen in Black and White
## From the Resurrected Spirit of Dixon Frye

"Ain't none of us perfect boy," then he laughed that way he did when he thought he was being cute, "except me and Jesus, of course."

I joined him and said, "And me."

We laughed together and I knew at that moment we had perfect simpatico. He smiled at my comment and said, "So, they's a good story about hypocrisy. You see, sometimes hypocrisy is part of a lie, and once there was a man who wanted to open a bar in this here small town. Now, I never drunk none in my life, but I see no difference in a bar and a church. They both trying to sell happiness, and neither do a good job of it in my opinion. Well, this here guy decided to open up his bar business, which was right opposite to a church. The church & its congregation started a campaign to block the bar from opening with petitions and they prayed daily against this here business, but work just kept on a going on that bar. However, when it was almost complete and was about to open a few days later, a strong lightning struck from a clear sky on the bar and it was burnt to the ground. The church folk were rather arrogant in their outlook after that saying God done answered their prayers. Well, the bar owner sued the church for a million dollars on the grounds that the church through its congregation with they's prayers caused the lightning strike."

"Now, the church in reply to the suit denied all

responsibility, but they's already been bragging about it all over town. So, what does they do? Before they's was saying how God answered the prayers. Now, they apparently are telling a lie as they say it wasn't God when they really believe it was. It was God's work, of course, until they got sued. So they's hypocrites of course and lie. That is the problem with Christians – hypocrisy."

"Now what's funny about his case is the bar owner was obviously lying 'bout believing in the power of prayer, but then the church decided it didn't believe in prayer's power. So, seems like the church is willing to engage in lies in order to protect itself, because it was bragging about the power of prayer before. Jesus said that you shall not bear false witness, which is just a fancy way of saying don't lie. Here is that hypocrisy again, the church was willing to lie in order to protect itself, but if 'un somebody else was lying it would be sinful. The judge actually decided the case in the bar owner's favour cause there were witnesses to the church bragging about their prayers causing the lightning strike. He only awarded the bar owner $50,000 though, but that was still a tidy sum and the church had to sell off everything and pay him, so the price of hypocrisy can be very high sometimes."

I nodded my head in agreement and said, "Yep, hypocrisy can have a high price alright, and so can lying."

## The Real Jesus Seen in Black and White
## From the Resurrected Spirit of Dixon Frye

I enjoyed a good rousing laugh with him and said, "Granddaddy, you remember when I was little you told me the story about the hypocritical cat?"

"Yep I do. That's a good 'un."

Feeling nostalgic for the old times when I was smaller, I said, "How about telling it again?"

Smiling at me, you could tell he was relishing my interest in his storytelling ability, and he began. "Once upon a time there was a troop of rats that used to live in holes by a river side. A certain cat often saw them going to and fro, and longed to have them to eat. But he was not strong enough to attack 'um all together; besides, that wouldn't have suited his purpose, because most of 'um would have run away. So he used to stand early in the morning, not far from their holes, with his face towards the sun, sniffing the air, and standing on one leg. The rats wondered why he did that, so one day theys all trooped up to him and asked the reason. First they asked him his name and he told 'um, 'holy is my name.' Then they asks him why he stands on one leg and he says 'cause if I stood on all four the earth would collapse from my weight.' Then they asks him why he kept his mouth open, and he says, 'cause I feed only on air, nothing else.' Then they asks him why he always faced the sun and he says, 'cause I worship the wonderful, the glorious sun.' Well, them rats says to themselves this is such a nice cat and a pious cat."

You could tell my grandfather was really getting into the story now. I was almost 11, but I was hanging on every word as if I was 5 or 6 and was hearing it for the first time. He continued. "After that, when they started out in the morning, the rats did not fail first to make their bow to the cat one by one, and to show their respect for his piety. You see, this was what the cat wanted. Every day, as they filed past, he waited till they passed and then when the last one pranced by, then like lightning he pounced on it and gobbled him up and stood there on one leg as before, licking his lips. The rats were really yummy. For a while all went well for the cat's plan; but at last the chief of the rats noticed that the troop seemed to grow smaller. Here and there he missed some familiar faces. He could not make it out; but at last a thought came into his mind, that perhaps the pious cat might know more about it than he chose to tell. Next day, he posted himself at the tail of the troop, where he could see everything that went on; and as the rats one by one bowed before the cat, he watched the cat closely. So, the observant rat decided to get at the end of the line of rats. As he came up, the cat prepared for his pounce. But Chief Rat was ready for him, and dodged out of the way. 'Aha!' says the Chief Rat, 'so that is your piety! Feeds on the air and worships the sun. What a humbug! And with one spring he was at the cat's throat with his sharp teeth. The other rats heard the scuffle, and came trooping back; and it was crunch and munch, till not a single piece remained of the hypocritical cat. And ever after the rats lived in peace and happiness and never ever did they fall for the lies of cats that acted like they were so pious but inside were deceitful and full of treachery."

I was really enjoying myself now, and could not resist excitedly blurting out, "You really hate hypocrites don't you granddaddy?"

"Well, hate may be too strong a word, but let's put it this away – I ain't got no use for 'um. Now, being a hypocrite is something down right common among politicians, and most of 'um claims to be religious, so's I see 'um as natural allies, politicians and Christians. They's one in the same when it comes to being hypocrites. Now, don't get me wrong, they's some good Christians who ain't hypocrites, but I don't find many, and they's a few politicians that's really trying to do right by the poor folks in this here country. Only problem is the bad 'uns seem to come to the top of the barrel. For some doggone reason the 'publicans seems to be the favoured party for Christians. Just don't make no sense though as the 'publicans ain't never once done nothing Jesus-like that I can see. My guess is Jesus would wash his hands with 'publcians and Democrats, if 'un he showed up agin."

## The Real Jesus Seen in Black and White
## From the Resurrected Spirit of Dixon Frye

"Real religion is what you do when the sermon is over. Anyway, most sermons is about all the evil in ya'. I don't need no preacher to tell me I'm evil. Truth is, I tries to be a good man, and frankly, I think I'm better than most preachers who tell me what not to do, then they go and do it they-selves. I just flat out never had no use for hypocrites. I guess that's why I ain't never cared for those 'publicans. They's the biggest pack of hypocrites I done ever seen. All they's talk about is Jesus this and Jesus that and they don't never do nothing Jesus woulda done. You think Jesus woulda voted agin' social security for old folks? *(He left out Medicare as it had not been passed, yet, but he certainly would have had a field day with the Republicans being against providing old people with healthcare.)* You think Jesus woulda said the returning GI's from that horrible war weren't entitled to education benefits and a home loan? You think Jesus woulda gone on a witch hunt after commies and tried to railroad 'um into the penitentiary when all they's want is a little human decency for all folks? You think Jesus woulda been for corporations and agin' people? You think Jesus woulda voted agin' any increase in the minimum wage so's the rich can keep more of they's money while poor folk struggle to put food on they's table? Them 'publicans oughtta change they's party name to the Pharisee's Party."

He sighed and continued. "Them 'publicans, most of 'um anyway, are always talking about love of God but they oughtta read the verse about 'If anyone says, I love God, and hates his brother, he is a liar; for he who does not love his brother whom he has seen cannot love God whom he has not seen.' Tell them 'publicans they's suppose to love the poor, supposed to love commies, suppose to love them Germans and Japanese we defeated in war. Go ahead and tell 'um and see what they do?"

"In Matthew, Jesus lays it out for hypocrites when he says, 'first take the log out of your own eye, and then you will see clearly to take the speck out of your brother's eye.' Jesus is saying stop judging others you hypocrite. In Matthew he also says, 'Judge not, that you be not judged. For with the judgment you pronounce you will be judged, and with the measure you use it will be measured to you. In James he says, 'people honour me with their lips, but their heart is far from me; in vain do they worship me, teaching as doctrines the commandments of men. What good is it, my brothers, if someone says he has faith but does not have works? Can that faith save him? If a brother or sister is poorly clothed and lacking in daily food, and one of you says to them to go in peace, be warmed and filled, without giving them the things needed for the body, what good is that? So also faith by itself, if it does not have works, is dead. Show me your faith apart from your works, and I will show you my faith by my works.' That's right from the Bible itself, but them

## The Real Jesus Seen in Black and White
## From the Resurrected Spirit of Dixon Frye

'publicans wouldn't know them scriptures if they bit 'um on the ass. I ain't no politician and I ain't no minister and I ain't no famous teacher of the Bible in some fancy school, but I tells you what, you start quoting the Bible to me and I can quote it right back at ya. I ain't much of a believer in fairy tales, but I read the biggest fairy tale of 'um all and I read it lots of times. Can't nobody out quote me on the Bible. I may not believe much of what's in it, but you better believe I know it, and I know it like the back of my hand, so don't start throwing that book in my face."

"Now, one of the biggest problems this here country's got is people posing as soemthin' they ain't. The Bible says, 'Beware of false prophets, who come to you in sheep's clothing but inwardly are ravenous wolves.' Right now my opinion of every one of them television preachers is they's false prophets. May be wrong about one or two, but I don't think so. That Billy Graham is a smooth operator, though, gotta give him credit for that, but you don't talk about being humble and build yourself a big mansion to live in. And that Oral Roberts, mark my words, that boy will be a super rich man one day and then he'll put aside all that healing baloney. These boys is building business empires. They's nothing but corporation executives hiding behind the pulpit. Them boys is the worst thing done ever happened to religion. They's selling people a bag of hope, but when peoples looks inside, ain't nothing there."

**The Real Jesus Seen in Black and White**
**From the Resurrected Spirit of Dixon Frye**

## CHAPTER 10
## THAT SCARES PEOPLE

*I am but a humble man*
*Lost in this thing called life.*
*For my grandson I do all I can*
*To somehow save him from strife.*
*Oh, let him see the truth*
*And avoid hypocrisy uncouth.*

*Make me tolerant and wise;*
*Incline my ears to hear him through;*
*Let him not stand with downcast eyes,*
*Fearing to trust me and be true.*
*Instruct me so that I may know*
*The way my grandson and I should go.*

*When he shall err, as often do I,*
*Or boyhood folly bids him stray,*
*Let me not into anger fly*
*And drive the good in him away.*
*Teach me to win his trust, that he*

### The Real Jesus Seen in Black and White
### From the Resurrected Spirit of Dixon Frye

*Shall keep no secret hid from me.*

*Strengthen me that I may be*
*A fit example for my grandson.*
*Grant he may never hear or see*
*A shameful deed that I have done.*
*However sorely I am tried,*
*Let me not undermine his pride.*

*In spite of years and temples grey,*
*Still let my spirit beat with joy;*
*Teach me to share in all his play*
*And be a comrade with my grand-boy.*
*Wherever we may chance to be,*
*Let him find happiness with me.*

*As his grandfather, now I've had my say*
*For manhood's strength and counsel wise;*
*Let me deal justly, day by day,*
*In all that being a grandfather implies.*
*Please keep my kindness so fit;*
*Let me not play the hypocrite!*

As a child, my world was often filled with anguish as living with an alcoholic father and a mother who was too afraid to challenge him could make my life difficult. Today, I blame neither of them, because I understand that we are all flawed. Their flaws did not mean I was not loved. It only meant, like all children, I was loved by imperfect human beings. Their imperfections have hopefully made me improve as a father and grandfather.

J. Wayne Frye

## The Real Jesus Seen in Black and White
## From the Resurrected Spirit of Dixon Frye

The anguish I often suffered was ameliorated by a saintly grandmother and a wise, though sometimes grumpy grandfather who offered guidance for life that has only recently, with age, begun to crystallize in my mind for what it was – unfettered love from a wise man who wanted me to grow and prosper as a human being free to think for myself, unencumbered with the restraining barriers placed by an intolerant society.

I am certainly far from a perfect human being, but thanks to my grandfather and father, I do strive to always let people know that what they see is what they get. I strive to avoid hypocrisy at all costs, but maybe my criticism of Christians for their hypocrisy is itself a form of hypocrisy, because I do sit in judgement of them just as Jesus sit in judgement of them. However, I am not Jesus.

The wise council of my grandfather pointed out to me that Jesus encountered hypocrisy several times during his earthly ministry, especially in the lives of the religious leaders of that day, and whenever he did he always condemned it severely. In fact, he repeatedly denounced the religious establishment by repeating the same strong rebuke over and over again: "Woe to you, scribes and Pharisees, hypocrites." My grandfather loved that quote and it is a quote I often use in describing those who act so pious but in reality lead lives far removed from that which was represented by the purity of Jesus.

## The Real Jesus Seen in Black and White
## From the Resurrected Spirit of Dixon Frye

My grandfather died a bit before the full-blown hippie movement of the late 1960's, but the beatniks were very similar as they saw through the banality of a life based on material possessions, and my grandfather saw the beatnik movement as something that Jesus would have supported. He actually said, "Hey, Jesus was the beatnik of his time. He lived outside of what was considered normal for those days. He didn't like authority, 'cause he saw it as controlling people's lives, not letting them reach they's full potential."

One evening, as we sat in the swing bundled up from the cold, I asked him a potent question. "Granddaddy, what you think about these beatniks going to church? You think any of them go?"

"Now, these here days we don't like nobody wearing long hair, scraggily beards and sandals in nice places. I mean if 'un you went to church wearing a pair of sandals and some long flowing robe them people in church would be disgusted. Yet, they's pictures hanging up in the church of a scraggily bearded man wearing a robe and sandals. Talk about hypocrisy. Them peoples just ain't got no clue about the real Jesus. Them beatnik folks done figured out you probably not gonna find Jesus in a church. My guess is Jesus wudn't be invited into a church, and I'd say he probably wudn't wanna go into one of them infernal places any way. He'd rather hang out with the people them churches is always throwing stones at."

## The Real Jesus Seen in Black and White
## From the Resurrected Spirit of Dixon Frye

"You see, hypocrisy is a form of deceit and Jesus done hated that. As Proverbs 12:22 says, 'The Lord detests lying lips, but he delights in men who are truthful.' In Proverbs 6 there is a list of deceitful actions that is considered awful. There are things the Lord hates, seven that are detestable to him: haughty eyes, a lying tongue, hands that shed innocent blood, a heart that devises wicked schemes, feet that are quick to rush into evil, a false witness who pours out lies and a man who stirs up trouble among brothers. So the Bible is very clear when it comes to telling us how God feels about any form of deceit, which would of course include hypocrisy."

I looked a little confused, so he continued. "A farmer once cut down a huge tree that was on his land. It looked good from the outside but he discovered that the heart of the tree was rotten. In other words, it was rotting from the inside out, but the outside still looked O.K. He looked closely at it and found a huge old nail. He figured that some years ago someone had drove it into the tree and it had caused the heart of the tree to rot. It was just a little thing that nail, but you see, the littlest thing can cause us to rot inside, cause us to turn our backs on good and only play at being good, show a good, even beautiful outside, but what is on the inside is a mess, an abomination. This is how it is with the life of the hypocritical person. His life becomes a hollow shell as his goodness withers and dies."

## The Real Jesus Seen in Black and White
## From the Resurrected Spirit of Dixon Frye

He could see that I still had questions, so he continued. "You remember that rattle snake me and Lloyd rescued you from out in that lot next to Bud Essick's place?"

"Yes," I replied.

"Hypocrisy is as deadly as that snake was, and you better always be afraid of it. It has bitten many people, and it may not a killed them instantly, but it killed them slowly over a long period of time as they started living shallow lives. Over the years hypocrisy has sunk its fangs into the lives of so many people and in so doing has poisoned their lives. You know where the word hypocrisy comes from boy?"

"No, Granddaddy."

"Well, I aint no scholar, but I made me a study of that word one time. Studied it in the dictionary real good. It comes from Greek. In Greek theatre an actor often played many roles in the same play by disguising himself with a series of masks. For example, he might come in from one side of the stage wearing a smiling mask, as he delivered one liners to make the people laugh. Then later, he'd come from the other side wearing a sad mask as he delivered sad lines. Well, this actor was called a hypocrite which meant someone with two or more faces. Over the years this Greek word took on special meaning and it wound up to mean two-faced, describing someone who said one thing and done another, someone who pretended to be something his or her actions didn't back up."

I was growing, not only in my knowledge of the Bible, which by this time I had read maybe twice, but thanks to my grandfather, I was growing in the true understanding of the Bible. He looked out at the expansive yard to his left, surveying all that he called his home. He said, "You see all that son? That is my world. I live here in this place and I don't thank God for it, cause I don't see God did any of the work that made this place what it is. Lot's of people have nice places, but they didn't do any of the work, so they don't appreciate what they got like I do. I built this house. I hand dug the well where we gets the water. I built the stable for the horses. I built the garage where your daddy works on cars. I built that smoke house where we cures our meat. I used to till the soil out there when I had corn planted. I worked hard for this here place. And ever time I drove a nail, cleaned up horse manure, moved some heavy boulders, I never once saw the lord help me with the burden. Now, I aint' blaming him if 'un he exists, but I sure didn't see him doing any of the work on this here place. This here place was built by Dixon Frye, your grandmother, and on occasion with the help of your uncle, aunt and daddy. What I am saying is that I did the work here, and if 'un I ever had help I was right there working alongside of that help."

## The Real Jesus Seen in Black and White
## From the Resurrected Spirit of Dixon Frye

He was about to get wound up now. I saw it coming. "Trouble is with this here world is people thinks they entitled if 'un they born into wealth. They tie up heavy loads and put them on other people's shoulders, but they themselves are not willing to lift a finger. As the Bible says, 'Everything they do is done for men to see: They make their phylacteries wide and the tassels on their garments long; they love the place of honour at banquets and the most important seats in the synagogues; they love to be greeted in the marketplaces and to have men call them Rabbi. Woe to you, teachers of the law and Pharisees, you hypocrites! You shut the kingdom of heaven in men's faces. You yourselves do not enter, nor will you let those enter who are trying to. Woe to you, teachers of the law and Pharisees, you hypocrites! You devour widows' houses and for a show make lengthy prayers. Therefore you will be punished more severely. Woe to you, teachers of the law and Pharisees, you hypocrites! You travel over land and sea to win a single convert, and when he becomes one, you make him twice as much a son of hell as you are. Woe to you, teachers of the law and Pharisees, you hypocrites! You give a tenth of your spices-mint, dill and cummin. But you have neglected the more important matters of the law like justice, mercy and faithfulness. You should have practiced the latter, without neglecting the former. You blind guides! You strain out a gnat but swallow a camel. Woe to you, teachers of the law and Pharisees,

## The Real Jesus Seen in Black and White
## From the Resurrected Spirit of Dixon Frye

you hypocrites! You clean the outside of the cup and dish, but inside they are full of greed and self-indulgence. Blind Pharisee! First clean the inside of the cup and dish, and then the outside also will be clean. Woe to you, teachers of the law and Pharisees, you hypocrites! You are like whitewashed tombs, which look beautiful on the outside but on the inside are full of dead men's bones and everything unclean. In the same way, on the outside you appear to people as righteous but on the inside you are full of hypocrisy and wickedness. Woe to you, teachers of the law and Pharisees, you hypocrites! You build tombs for the prophets and decorate the graves of the righteous. And you say, 'If we had lived in the days of our forefathers, we would not have taken part with them in shedding the blood of the prophets.' So you testify against yourselves that you are the descendants of those who murdered the prophets. Fill up, then, the measure of the sin of your forefathers! You snakes! You brood of vipers! How will you escape being condemned to hell?"

I sat in awe as he continued. "Jesus didn't pussy-foot around. He said it like it was. He knew the damage that their poisonous hypocritical actions caused. These Pharisees pretended to be spiritually strong but were weaklings in their hearts. They sounded righteous but was empty of spiritual substance. And with all this two-facedness they had pushed people away from God, rather than toward him. Same thing goes on today."

## The Real Jesus Seen in Black and White
## From the Resurrected Spirit of Dixon Frye

My grandmother came to the front door, looked out at us, and seeing Dixon was in one of his philosophical moods, closed the door and went back inside. My grandfather never missed a beat in his rhythmic song damning hypocrisy. "Today boy, television and the pulpits are full of hypocrites who are busy telling people what not to do, but they doing the very things they say is sinning, just like the Pharisees of Jesus' day who, did not practice what they preached. But you know, we mustn't fall into the trap of thinking that pastors and other spiritual leaders are the only ones who allow theyselves to become hypocritical. Ain't it funny how we praise old George Washington as the father of this here country, and he married a widow woman for her money, used to have to be rolled home in a wheelbarrow when he got so drunk at the local pub he couldn't walk. And what about all them slaves he owned. I read where he was the biggest slave holder in America. I mean, talk about hypocrisy."

"Think about it. We all fall for the lies we's told by people we's supposed to respect. We's taught to respect teachers and ministers, but what makes them folks so special, when they feeding us lies? You member when you challenged that Sunday School teacher? All hell broke loose cause you was just showing a little intelligence, but they's afraid of intelligent people, cause intelligent people ask why and don't just do as they's told. That scares people."

**The Real Jesus Seen in Black and White
From the Resurrected Spirit of Dixon Frye**

## CHAPTER 11
## THE BLACK VEIL

*Why do we spurn reality,
and seek solace in illusion?
Where does reality end
and illusion truly begin?
Why do we exchange the truth,
for a touch of easy fantasy?
Can we not see the control
exercised by what we are told?
Why do we shield hypocrisy,
under the guise of practicality?
Why do we restrain ourselves,
easily writing off truth,
as just a little lunacy?
Why do we pretend,
knowing we are but only pretending?
Why do we choose to move apart
for the apparent better,
leaving behind the other in that graveyard
of dark collective shadows?*

J. Wayne Frye               159

## The Real Jesus Seen in Black and White
## From the Resurrected Spirit of Dixon Frye

Often, I sat in absolute amazement at my grandfather's ability to easily quote the Bible verbatim. This man with a third grade education was a fountain of knowledge. What Harvard professor of theology could hold his own with Worth Buren "Dixon" Frye, a man who feared no one? Who bowed before no man, be he ignoble, base, degraded, dwarfed, inferior or an exalted king upon a throne of gold. My admiration was absolute for this humble, simple, direct-talking man. He, to me, was becoming a giant in a kingdom of knowledge.

One Sunday afternoon, after returning from "down the country" where I had attended Sunday School that morning, I sat awaiting the arrival of my mom and dad to pick me up after a great weekend with my grandparents. As always, I sat in the swing beside my grandfather as we gently swayed back and forth. That day in Sunday School we had talked about proverbs. I mentioned to my grandfather that I enjoyed reading proverbs, because they were easier to understand than a lot of the other parts of the Bible. Of course, his favourite proverbs dealt with hypocrisy. He could not resist a discourse. "You see, hypocrisy is a form of deceit and God hates all forms of falsehood. As, Proverbs 12:22 says, 'The Lord detests lying lips, but he delights in men who are truthful.' So the Bible is very clear when it comes to telling us how God feels about any form of deceit, which would of course include hypocrisy.

## The Real Jesus Seen in Black and White
## From the Resurrected Spirit of Dixon Frye

1 John 4:8 says that God is love, but some make the mistake of thinking that God is only love. Jesus said, 'I am the way, the truth, and the life.' And, in John 16:13, the Holy Spirit is called the Spirit of Truth. So, just as God defines what it means to be good, holy, and pure; he also defines what it means to be true. And because he does, he can't tolerate being false. Now, if 'un you got allergies you try to stay away from things what causes you to get stopped up and sneeze. I's allergic to hypocrisy, so I stays away from people who are hypocrites as much as I can. That's why you don't see me in church much. I just don't cotton too all that holier than thou stuff, and I don't believe most of them fairy tales anyway. I mean I'm an adult, not some kid who supposed to be afeared of that mean old devil."

Looking up admirably at him, I said, "Well, I am not sure I believe either granddaddy. I sure don't believe in fairy tales."

"Well boy, I am just telling you my opinion. You gotta decide for yourself what you believe and disbelief."

"The thing you hate most is hypocrisy isn't it granddaddy?"

"It is Wayne. Hypocrisy also poisons us. I means, the more we pretend to be what we ain't, the easier it is for us to do so. And the more we do this, the more we pretend, the more we begin to lose our real selves. Hey, I am who I am. Might not like me, and that's O.K., but what you sees is what you gets."

"So, you saying that hypocrisy is an evil then?"

"As Paul says in Romans 12:9 'Love must be sincere.' We need to trust one another. Now, when you been lied to so many times by folks, ain't it hard to trust 'um?"

"Yes."

Lying makes people not trust one another and hypocrisy destroys trust. Paul told the Ephesians, that we must put off falsehood and live truthfully with our neighbours. Hypocrisy is like a cancer. It grows and grows and can destroy people, and it is destroying the church. People's turning away from the church. Smart people that is, who see through all them lies."

"So, you are saying that he church is actually killing itself by allowing all this hypocrisy."

"Yes, it is, boy. But that may be good."

"What you mean, good?"

"Well, church as I sees it don't do nobody no good but the church itself. Remember, hypocrisy is basically pretending, acting like something we're not. And we pretend and hide our true selves behind masks because we is so afeared of life that we have to think they's something after this here life. You see, fear don't prevent death. It prevents life."

"So, you saying most people are just putting on an act?"

"Think Wayne. When you goes into some fancy place do you act different? Course you do. Why? Cause you think you have to be good enough to be there. You may be poor, so you acts rich-like to make people think you belong. Now, you really wanna see people acting, pretending they is what they ain't. Just go to church. Each of us does his best to hide behind a shield. We may be silent cause we are afeared that what we say might make us seem dumb, or we might try silver-tongued chit-chat to acts like we ere smart. We's all wearing masks. In the church many mask themselves with spirituality. They quote Bible verses or speak of having deep peace or of God being in control when the truth is inside they are all scared because they feel like they's lives are out of control! Truth is most people's afraid of life, scared to death of it. They need hope that there's something better."

"So, you saying church is for people who are afraid of life?"

## The Real Jesus Seen in Black and White
## From the Resurrected Spirit of Dixon Frye

"Mostly boy that is correct. If you wear a mask, if you get really good at figuring out what other people wants and then delivering it, you are all show but don't got no substance. That means you are always hiding behind a mask. Nobody ever really knows the real you. Children is the ones who don't usually hide behind a mask until they's get older, then they do it too. I mean you see somebody making fun of a boy who is a sissy, and you join in calling him names. Why? Cause you putting on that mask to fit in. You know you's doing wrong, but you do it so you won't be like that boy, won't be called a sissy. Just like going to church to prove you ere a good person. All show, all show."

"I have done that granddaddy, but usually I stand up for the kids being picked on, cause I feel sorry for them. I asked myself how I would feel if I was the one being picked on, the one being made fun of."

"That's cause you got a good heart boy. You know that them very things people act like is awful, they does them things when everybody's back is turned. As we get older we learns to wear masks: to look confident when our hearts are scared, to look pious when our hearts are full of temptation or guilt. So, hypocrisy poisons our relationship with good; it poisons us; it poisons our friends and families. Living a lie is not really living."

164 J. Wayne Frye

## The Real Jesus Seen in Black and White
## From the Resurrected Spirit of Dixon Frye

He took a deep breathe and said, "You know what? I been called an atheist by some peoples, and you know what that is, right?"

"I do granddaddy, but I'd say you are more of an agnostic."

"True Wayne, that is a better description of what I am. You know what the single most cause of atheism in the world today is? It is Christians, who acknowledge Jesus with their lips but walk out of the church doors and deny him in everything they do."

"We are all really searching for the same thing aren't we granddaddy?"

"We are. Trouble is we all wants meaning to life, but my opinion they ain't much meaning to it other than love, which is what we got here on this here porch right now. A famous poet once said: 'It is all in vain to preach the truth, to the eager ears of trusting youth, if whenever the lad is standing by, he sees you cheat and he hears you lie.' That there is hypocrisy. It's like me telling you not to lie, then I lie to you bout the Easter Bunny, Santa Claus or believing in God."

"How come you can't talk to Christians sensibly, granddaddy? Get them to acknowledge that they could be wrong. That all they believe could just be one big fairy tale?"

## The Real Jesus Seen in Black and White
## From the Resurrected Spirit of Dixon Frye

"Wayne, them Christians is too hard-headed to even talk too sensibly. Arguing with a person who has turned his back on reason is like giving medicine to a dead man. Just ain't gonna do no good. Them Christians been brainwashed by them devil preachers, been took-over by what I'd call pure insanity of reason. They is worse than kids when you try to challenge they's belief in fairy tales. I mean if 'un you told them that pink elephants was seen flying down town at the city hall, they'd all laugh at you, but tell 'um that some 600 year old man built an ark and put two of every creature on earth in a boat that was smaller than the Titanic and they's start shouting amen. Tell 'um that you seen an eight armed woman with four heads floating above that same city hall calling people to heaven and they laugh they's heads off. But tell 'um that some man done lived in the belly of a whale, and they'll jump up and down and shout halleluiah. I mean these people is just plum crazy. You can't reason with a crazy man in an insane asylum, and that's what a church is. It's an insane asylum for them folks that ain't been committed yet. I mean if 'un you went around Clyde Steed's Texaco saying you done been talking to God and he told ya to build an ark for all the animals in the world, or you just jumped out of the belly of a whale where you done lived for a week, they'd call the guys in the white coats to lock you up 'fore you harmed somebody. But tell them a story from the Bible and they all become little children agin."

## The Real Jesus Seen in Black and White
## From the Resurrected Spirit of Dixon Frye

We were both laughing now as he managed to blurt out, "You ever hear the story of the dark veil?"

Smiling, because I knew he was anxious to share it with me, I said, "No I haven't, but I have sneaking suspicion I am about to hear it."

"They was this village where the church sexton stood on the porch of a meeting-house, pulling busily at the bell-rope. The old people of the village came stooping along the street. Children, skipped along merrily beside their parents in their Sunday finest. Fine-looking bachelors looked sideways out of the corner of their eyes at the pretty girls all dressed up, and fancied that the Sabbath sunshine made them prettier than on week days. When the throng had mostly streamed into the porch, the sexton began to toll the bell, keeping his eye on the Reverend Mr. Hooper's door. The first glimpse of the clergyman's figure was the signal for the bell to cease its summoning. Suddenly a strange looking figure appeared and it wasn't their parson they all thought. But then they saw him closer and it was their parson. Now Parson Hooper was a gentlemanly person of about thirty, though still a bachelor, was dressed with clerical neatness, as if a careful wife had starched his collar band, and brushed the weekly dust from his Sunday's garb. There was but one thing remarkable in his appearance. Over his forehead, and hanging down over his face, so low as to be

## The Real Jesus Seen in Black and White
## From the Resurrected Spirit of Dixon Frye

shaken by his breath, Mr. Hooper had on a black veil. On a nearer view it seemed to consist of two folds of cloth, which totally concealed his features, except the mouth and chin. With this gloomy shade before him, good Mr. Hooper walked onward, at a slow and quiet pace, stooping somewhat, and looking on the ground, nodding kindly to those of his parishioners who still waited on the meeting-house steps. But so wonder-struck were they that his greeting hardly met with a return greeting at all. The people were absolutely bewildered."

I had never heard this story before, so I was following each word with grand interest, and you could tell my grandfather enjoyed my interest as he continued. "The sexton uttered to someone that he wasn't sure it was Pastor Hopper behind the veil. An old women angrily said that he had a lot of nerve to show up looking like that and that he had changed himself into something awful, only by hiding his face. Another parishioner said that the parson had apparently gone mad. There was a stirring of discontent among the congregation. Few could refrain from twisting their heads towards the door; many stood upright, and turned directly about; while several little boys clambered upon the seats and come down again with a terrible racket. There was a general bustle, a rustling of the women's gowns and shuffling of the men's feet, and the silence of the place was so intense you could have easily heard a pin drop on

J. Wayne Frye

the floor. But Mr. Hooper appeared not to notice the concerned nature of his congregation. He entered the sanctuary with an almost noiseless step, bent his head mildly to the pews on each side, and bowed as he passed his oldest parishioner, a white-haired man of almost 100 who occupied an arm-chair in the centre of the aisle. It was strange to observe how slowly this venerable man became conscious of something singular in the appearance of his pastor. He seemed not fully to partake of the prevailing wonder, till Mr. Hooper had ascended the stairs, and showed himself in the pulpit, face to face with his congregation, except for the black veil. That mysterious emblem was never once withdrawn. It shook with his measured breath, as he read from the Psalms. Ah, the veil caused a wall-like barrier between him and the holy page, as he read the Scriptures; and while he prayed, the veil lay heavily on his uplifted countenance. Did he seek to hide himself from the God of whom he was speaking? Such was the effect of this simple piece of cloth, that more than one woman of delicate nerves was forced to leave the meeting-house. Yet, perhaps the pale-faced congregation was almost as fearful a sight to the minister, as his black veil to them. Mr. Hooper had the reputation of a good preacher, but not an energetic one: he strove to win his people heavenward by mild, persuasive influences, rather than to drive them thither by the thunders of God's word. The sermon which he now delivered was marked by the same

## The Real Jesus Seen in Black and White
## From the Resurrected Spirit of Dixon Frye

characteristics of style and manner as the general series of his pulpit oratory. But there was something, either in the sermon itself, or in the imagination of the listeners, which made it greatly the most powerful effort that they had ever heard from their pastor's lips. It was tinged, rather more darkly than usual, with the gentle gloom of Mr. Hooper's temperament. The subject had reference to secret sin, and those sad mysteries which we hide from our nearest and dearest, and would conceal from our own consciousness, even forgetting that God can detect them. A subtle power was breathed into his words. Each member of the congregation, the most innocent girl, and the man of hardened breast, felt as if the preacher had crept upon them, behind his awful veil, and discovered their most inner deeds or thoughts. Many spread their clasped hands on their bosoms. There was nothing terrible in what Mr. Hooper said, at least, no violence; and yet, with every tremor of his melancholy voice, the hearers quaked. They were so frightened that they longed for a breath of wind to blow aside the veil, almost believing that a stranger's face would be discovered, though the form, gesture, and voice were those of Mr. Hooper. Yes, there was a darkness that was hanging over this little church."

I had an intensity in my manner as I hung on each world uttered by my grandfather. I stared at him with anticipation of what was to come, as he took slight pause and gathered his breath.

## The Real Jesus Seen in Black and White
## From the Resurrected Spirit of Dixon Frye

"At the close of the services, the people hurried out filled with confusion, eager to communicate their pent-up amazement, and conscious of lighter spirits the moment they lost sight of the black veil. Some gathered in little circles, huddled closely together, with their mouths all whispering in the centre; some went homeward alone, wrapt in silent meditation; some talked loudly, and profaned the minister for doing something so frightful to all. A few shook their heads, indicating that they could penetrate the mystery; while one or two affirmed that there was no mystery at all, but only that Mr. Hooper's eyes were so weakened by the midnight reading, as to require a cover. After a brief interval, forth came good Mr. Hooper also, in the rear of his flock. Turning his veiled face from one group to another, he paid due reverence to them, saluted the middle aged with kind dignity as their friend and spiritual guide, greeted the young with mingled authority and love, and laid his hands on the little children's heads to bless them. Such was always his custom on the Sabbath day. Strange and bewildered looks repaid him for his courtesy. None, as on former occasions, aspired to the honour of walking by their pastor's side. Old Squire Saunders, doubtless by an accidental lapse of memory, neglected to invite Mr. Hooper to his table, where the good clergyman had been wont to bless the food, almost every Sunday since his arrival in the village. He returned, therefore, to the parsonage, and, at the moment of closing the door, was observed to look back upon the people, all of whom had their eyes upon the minister. A sad smile gleamed faintly from beneath the black veil, and flickered about his mouth, glimmering as he disappeared into the parsonage."

"How strange thought one lady that a simple black veil, such as any woman might wear on her hat, should become such a terrible thing on Mr. Hooper's face! Yes, one man even came out and said it aloud that the man had simply gone mad. It was this man who said that the black veil did more than cover the pastor's face. It covered his intentions, and what were his intentions? Were they dark and sinister like the veil?"

My grandfather slowed the sway of the swing as he continued. "One woman said she would never be alone with him again for she feared he was hiding some devilish intent behind that veil. The evening service was attended with similar circumstances. At its conclusion, the bell tolled for the funeral of a young lady. The relatives and friends were assembled in the house, and the more distant acquaintances stood about the door, speaking of the good qualities of the deceased, when their talk was interrupted by the appearance of Mr. Hooper, still covered with his black veil. The minister stepped into the room where the corpse was laid, and bent over the coffin, to take a last farewell of his deceased parishioner. As he stooped, the veil hung straight down from his forehead, so that, if her eyelids had not been closed forever, the dead woman might have seen his face. Could Mr. Hooper be fearful of her glance, that he so hastily caught back the black veil? A person who watched this incident between the dead and living, later said at the instant when the clergyman's features were disclosed, the corpse had slightly shuddered, rustling the shroud, as if she had started to breath again. A superstitious old woman was the only witness of this incident. From the coffin, Mr. Hooper passed into the chamber of the mourners, and thence to the head of the staircase, to make the funeral prayer. It was a tender and heart-dissolving prayer, full of sorrow, yet filled with celestial hopes, that the music of a heavenly harp, swept by the fingers of the dead, seemed faintly to be heard among the saddest there. The people trembled, though they but darkly understood him when he prayed that they, and himself, and all of mortal race, might be ready, as he trusted this young maiden had been, for the dreadful hour that should snatch the veil from their faces. The bearers went heavily forth, and the mourners followed, saddening the entire street, with the dead before them, and Mr. Hooper in his black veil behind. As they walked, one woman kept looking back and told her mother, who was beside her, that she sensed the minister was walking with someone, though he appeared alone. It was as if there was a spirit beside him. Yes, he was with the dead woman, and he had his hand by his side as if he was holding someone's hand. Yet, no one was there."

### The Real Jesus Seen in Black and White
### From the Resurrected Spirit of Dixon Frye

Now, by this time I had a tingling sensation going up and down my spine. This was definitely one of his better stories, and he, no doubt, like the Bible, had it memorized as his grammar and diction were purer and more accurate than usual.

"That night, the handsomest couple in the village were to be joined in wedlock. Though seemingly a sad man, Mr. Hooper had cheerfulness for such occasions, which often excited a sympathetic smile where livelier merriment would have been thrown away. There was no quality of his disposition which made him more beloved than this. The company at the wedding awaited his arrival with impatience, trusting that the strange awe, which had gathered over him throughout the day, would now be dispelled. But such was not the result. When Mr. Hooper came, the first thing that their eyes rested on was the same horrible black veil, which had added deeper gloom to the funeral, and could signal nothing but evil to the wedding. Such was its immediate effect on the guests that a cloud seemed to have rolled from beneath the black veil, and dimmed the light of the candles. The bridal pair stood up before the minister, but the bride's cold fingers quivered in the hand of the bridegroom, and her deathlike paleness caused a whisper that the maiden who had been buried a few hours before was come from her grave to be married. Never in the history of the village was a wedding so dismal."

## The Real Jesus Seen in Black and White
## From the Resurrected Spirit of Dixon Frye

I was hanging on every word now as he continued. "After performing the ceremony, Mr. Hooper raised a glass of wine to his lips, wishing happiness to the new-married couple. At that instant, catching a glimpse of his figure in the looking-glass, the black veil involved his own spirit in the horror with which it overwhelmed all others. His frame shuddered, his lips grew white, he spit the wine upon the carpet, and rushed forth into the darkness. The black veil had captured his soul many felt. The next day, the whole village talked of little else than Parson Hooper's black veil. That, and the mystery concealed behind it, supplied a topic for discussion between acquaintances meeting in the street, and good women gossiping at their open windows. It was the first item of news that the tavern-keeper told to his guests. The children babbled of it on their way to school. One imitative little boy covered his face with an old black handkerchief, thereby so freighting his playmates that the panic seized upon one and all, causing mass hysteria."

My grandfather purposefully paused, stopping the story so that I would be even more enthralled. I looked to my left and there by the front door to the porch stood my grandmother, who was equally interested in a story that she had obviously not heard him utter in all the years they had been together. She eased through the doorway, moved to her rocker, never taking her eyes off him as she said, "Go on Dixon. Go on."

## The Real Jesus Seen in Black and White
## From the Resurrected Spirit of Dixon Frye

You could see the pleasure my grandfather took in getting our rapt-like attention with his tale. With just a tinge of a smile, he continued, as my grandmother eased into her rocker. "It was remarkable that of all the busybodies and unmannerly people in the parish, not one ventured to put the plain question to Mr. Hooper about why he was wearing this black veil. Hitherto, whenever there appeared the slightest call for such interference, he had never lacked advisers, nor shown himself adverse to be guided by their judgment. No individual among his parishioners chose to make the black veil a subject of friendly discussion. There was a feeling of dread, neither plainly confessed nor carefully concealed, which caused each to shift the responsibility upon another, till at length it was decided that someone should contact the District Bishop and let him know what was going on. Never did an embassy so ill discharge its duties. The bishop received them with friendly courtesy, but became silent, after they were seated, leaving to his visitors the whole burden of introducing their important business. The topic, it might be supposed, was obvious enough. There was the black veil swathed round Mr. Hooper's forehead, and concealing every feature above his placid mouth, on which, at times, they could perceive the glimmering of a saddened smile. But that piece of veil, to their imagination, seemed to hang down before his heart, the symbol of a fearful secret between him and them. Were the veil but cast aside, they might

J. Wayne Frye

speak freely of it, but not till then. Thus they sat a considerable time, speechlessly confused, and shrinking uneasily from their task, which they felt was itself a burden upon the bishop. Finally, the bishop pronounced the matter too weighty to be handled just by him, it would require a meeting of the synod council."

My grandmother was now as intensely interested as I was. She leaned toward Dixon, her eyes focused and her mind obviously looking for just where this was leading.

Grandfather sighed and said, "But there was one person in the village not appalled by the awe with which the black veil had impressed all beside herself. When the people returned without an explanation from the bishop, only a promise it would be explored further, she, with the calm energy of her character, determined to chase away the strange cloud that appeared to be settling round Mr. Hooper, every moment more darkly than before. Now as the woman to whom he was engaged, it should be her privilege to know what the black veil concealed. She had ignored it for the week that it had been the subject of everyone's concern, but decided to broach the subject with a direct simplicity, which made the task easier both for him and her. After he had seated himself, she fixed her eyes steadfastly upon the veil, but could discern nothing of the dreadful gloom that had so overwhelmed others: it was but a double fold of

## The Real Jesus Seen in Black and White
## From the Resurrected Spirit of Dixon Frye

thin mesh material, hanging down from his forehead to his mouth, and slightly stirring with his breath. She saw nothing sinister about it. It was nothing more than a slight covering of his face. Perhaps he had some rash, something he felt might offend people's sensibilities. She said to him in a very direct manner to please tell her why he wore the veil. He, without hesitation, said to her that there would be an hour to come when all of us shall cast aside our veils. He begged her not to seek further knowledge until that time. She agreed, but asked when the time would be. He said, 'Elizabeth, I have taken a vow that I cannot break. Know, then, this veil is a type and a symbol, and I am bound to wear it forever, both in light and darkness, in solitude and before the gaze of multitudes, and as with strangers, so with my familiar friends. No mortal eye will see it withdrawn. This dismal shade must separate me from the world: even you, Elizabeth, can never come behind it!' Oh, how defeated she felt as she loved him so, but to never look upon his face again. It seemed too much. She asked him what horrible affliction had befallen him that he should have to hide his face forever. He told her that he had sorrows like all others in life, and that he was just putting his sorrows behind a black veil. She told that him being beloved and respected as he was, there might be whispers that he hides his face under the consciousness of secret sin. She begged him for the sake of his exalted position to remove this plight on his character."

## The Real Jesus Seen in Black and White
## From the Resurrected Spirit of Dixon Frye

My grandmother could not help but interrupt. "Yes, he should have listened to her, but you men are too stubborn. I bet he didn't."

Smiling at my beloved Grandmother, Dixon said, "Of course not. The colour rose into her cheeks as she recounted the nature of the rumours that were already swirling about the village. But Mr. Hooper's mildness did not forsake him. He gave her a sad smile from beneath the veil. He told her, 'If I hide my face for sorrow, there is cause enough, and if I cover it for secret sin, what mortal might not do the same?' Thus did he resist all her pleadings and at length Elizabeth sat silent. For a few moments she appeared lost in thought, considering, probably, what new methods might be tried to withdraw her lover from so dark a fantasy, which, if it had no other meaning, was perhaps a symptom of mental disease. Though of a firmer character than his own, the tears rolled down her cheeks. But, in an instant, as it were, a new feeling took the place of sorrow: her eyes were fixed suddenly on the black veil, when suddenly its terrors fell around her. She arose, and stood trembling before him and turned to leave the room. He rushed forward and caught her arm, pleading with her to have patience with him if she indeed loved him. He begged her not to desert him, though this veil must be between them forever on this earth. He, with great emotion said, 'Be mine, and hereafter there shall be no veil over my face, no darkness between our souls! It is but a

## The Real Jesus Seen in Black and White
## From the Resurrected Spirit of Dixon Frye

mortal veil. It is not for eternity! You know not how lonely I am, and how frightened, to be alone behind my black veil. Do not leave me in this misery forever!' She pleaded for him to lift the veil just once and look into her face, but he said that he could not. She lowered her head and told him farewell."

My grandfather stopped for awhile, and cleared his throat as my grandmother, now as enthralled as I was, said, "Go on Dixon. Go on. Did he leave her?"

Clearing his throat one more time, he said, "She withdrew her arm from his grasp, and slowly departed, pausing at the door, to give one long gaze back that seemed almost to penetrate the mystery of the black veil. But, even amid his grief, Mr. Hooper smiled to think that only a material emblem had separated him from happiness, though the horrors, which it shadowed forth, must be drawn darkly between the fondest of lovers. From that time no attempts were made to remove Mr. Hooper's black veil, or, by a direct appeal, to discover the secret which it was supposed to hide. By persons who claimed some superiority in these matters, it was reckoned merely an eccentric whim, such as often mingles with the sober actions of men otherwise rational, and tinges them all with its own semblance of insanity. But when even the church seemed to ignore the pleas from the villagers as they could see no honest reason to remove him from his duties just because of the veil, he walked the streets with no peace of mind, so conscious was he that the gentle and timid would turn aside to avoid him. Eventually he felt compelled to give up his customary walk at sunset to the burial ground; for when he leaned over the gate, there would always be faces behind the gravestones, peeping at his black veil. A fable went the rounds that the stare of the dead people drove him crazy. It grieved him, to the very depth of his kind heart, to observe how the children fled from his approach, breaking up their merriest sports, while his melancholy figure was yet afar off. Their instinctive dread caused him to feel the threads of the black veil were now around his neck, strangling the life from him. In truth, his own hatred of the veil was known to be so great, that he never willingly passed before a mirror, nor stooped to drink at a still fountain, lest, he would see the veil himself and be repulsed and horrified by it. This was what made some believe that Mr. Hooper's conscience tortured him for some great horrible crime he had committed. Thus, from beneath the black veil, there was a cloud which overwhelmed the poor minister, so that love or sympathy could never reach him. It was said that ghosts haunted him there under the black veil. With misery abounding, he walked continually in the shadow of unhappiness, groping darkly within his own soul, or gazing through a medium that saddened the whole world. Even the wayward wind, it was believed, respected his dreadful secret, and never blew aside the veil. But still good Mr. Hooper sadly smiled at those who passed him by, always uttering a friendly greeting that was never returned."

My grandmother said, "My, my what a sad man he must have been. My heart aches for him."

I almost shouted, "Mine too."

We were mesmerized as granddaddy continued. "Among all its bad influences, the black veil had the one desirable effect, of making its wearer a very efficient minister. By the aid of his mysterious emblem, for there was no other apparent cause, he became a man of awful power over souls that were in agony for sin. His converts always regarded him with a dread peculiar to themselves, figuratively affirming, that before he brought them to see the light, they had been with him behind the black veil. Its gloom, indeed, enabled him to sympathize with all dark afflictions. Dying sinners cried aloud for Mr. Hooper, and would not yield their breath till he appeared; though ever, as he stooped to whisper consolation, they shuddered at the veiled face so near their own. Such were the terrors of the black veil when death came calling. Strangers came long distances to attend service at his church, with the mere idle purpose of gazing at his figure, because it was forbidden them to behold his face. But many were made to shudder in fear. Once, Mr.

## The Real Jesus Seen in Black and White
## From the Resurrected Spirit of Dixon Frye

Hooper was appointed to preach the election sermon of a local politician who had been elected to state-wide office. Despite the fear of that black veil, he was sought after, but was it for the good or for the evil the people feared? In this manner, Mr. Hooper spent a long life, unapproachable due to fear, shrouded in dismal suspicions; kind and loving, though unloved, and dimly feared; a man apart from men, shunned by one and all, but ever summoned to their aid in mortal anguish. As years wore on, he acquired a name throughout the land where he was. They called him, though not catholic, Father Hooper. Nearly all his original parishioners, who were of mature age when he first put on the black veil, had been borne away by the angel of death: he had one congregation in the church, and a more crowded one in the churchyard; and having wrought so late into the evening, and done his work so well, it was now good Father Hooper's turn for eternal rest."

I watched as my soft-hearted Grandmother gently wiped tears from her eyes, and my own eyes were becoming moist.

"Several persons were visible by the shaded candle-light, in the death chamber of the old minister. Natural connections with anyone, he had none. But there was an unmoved physician, seeking only to mitigate the last pangs of the patient whom he could not save. There were the deacons, and other eminently pious members of his church. There, also, was the Reverend Mr. Clark, a young and zealous minister, who had ridden in haste to pray by the bedside of the expiring minister. There was the nurse, whose calm affection had helped ease his suffering, and she would not leave his side at the dying hour. Ah, but she was no real nurse, she was just someone who cared for him deeply. It was his dear Elizabeth! And there lay frail, the skeleton-like head of good Father Hooper upon the death pillow, with the black veil still about his face that reached down over his face, so that each more difficult gasp of his faint breath caused it to stir. All through life that piece of material had hung between him and the world: it had separated him from cheerful brotherhood and a woman's love, and kept him in that saddest of all prisons, his own heart; and still it lay upon his face, as if to deepen the gloom of his darksome chamber, and shade him from the sunshine of eternity."

Now, my grandmother was actually crying, and I began to weep with her. Through it all, my grandfather remained stoic, not wavering in his commitment to weave this tale of woe. "For some time previous, Hopper's mind had been confused, wavering between the past and the present, and hovering forward, as it were, at intervals, into the indistinctness of the world to come. There had been feverish turns, which tossed him from side to side, and wore away what little strength he had. But in his most difficult struggles, and in the

J. Wayne Frye

## The Real Jesus Seen in Black and White
## From the Resurrected Spirit of Dixon Frye

wildest imaginations, when no other thought retained its sober influence, he still showed an awful solicitude lest the black veil should slip aside. Even if his bewildered soul could have forgotten, there was a faithful woman at his pillow, who, with averted eyes, would have covered that aged face, which she had last beheld in his youth. At length the death-stricken old man lay quietly in mental and bodily exhaustion, with a lowering pulse, and breath that grew fainter and fainter, except when a long, deep inspiration seemed to prelude the flight of his spirit. The young minister approached the bedside and said, 'Pastor Hopper, the time for your release is at hand. Are you ready for the lifting of the veil that shuts in time from eternity?' Father Hooper at first replied merely by a feeble motion of his head; then, apprehensive, perhaps, that his meaning might be doubtful, he exerted himself to speak. His words were faint, barely discernable, 'Yea,' said he, in faint gasps, 'my soul hath a patient weariness until that veil be lifted.' He gasped for breath now."

My Grandmother was actually wiping tears now, as my Grandfather continued. "The young reverend told him that it was fitting that a man so given to prayer, of such a blameless example, holy in deed and thought, so far as mortal judgment may pronounce; it simply was not fitting that a reverend in the church should leave a shadow on his memory, that might blacken a life so pure? He pleaded with him to allow the veil of eternity be greeted by casting aside the black veil of this life. And thus speaking, the young reverend bent forward to reveal the mystery of so many years. But, exerting a sudden burst of energy that made all the beholders stand aghast, Mr. Hooper snatched both his hands from beneath the bedclothes, and pressed them strongly on the black veil, determined to struggle, if the young minister dared lift the veil on a dying man. He shouted, 'never! Never on this earth shall I raise this black veil.' Then the young minister admonished him, saying that he should not pass into judgment with a horrible crime on his soul, that the black veil must be lifted."

Dixon shifted his position, as you could tell the end was drawing near. "Now the young minister really lost it. He called him an evil, dark old man with no love of God. Father Hooper's breath heaved; it rattled in his throat; but, with a mighty effort, grasping forward with his hands, he caught hold of life, and held back death till he should speak. He even raised himself in bed; and there he sat, shivering with the arms of death around him, while the black veil hung down, awful at that last moment, in the gathered terrors of a lifetime, and yet the faint, sad smile, so often there, now seemed to glimmer and dance with delight, and linger on Hooper's lips. 'Why do you tremble at me alone?' he cried, turning his veiled face round the circle of pale spectators. 'Tremble also at each

## The Real Jesus Seen in Black and White
## From the Resurrected Spirit of Dixon Frye

other! Have men avoided me, and women shown no pity, and children screamed and fled, only for my black veil? What, but the mystery which it typifies, has made this piece of cloth so awful? When the friend shows his inmost heart to his friend; the lover to his best beloved; when man does not vainly shrink from the eye of his Creator, loathsomely treasuring up the secret of his sin; then deem me a monster, for the symbol beneath which I have lived and die! I look around me, and, low and behold, on every face I see a black veil!' While his observers shrank from one another, in mutual excitement, Hooper fell back upon his pillow, a veiled corpse, with a faint smile lingering on the lips. Still veiled, they laid him in his coffin, and his veiled corpse was borne to the grave. The grass of many years has sprung up and withered on that grave, the burial stone is moss-grown, and good Mr. Hooper's face is dust; but awful is still the thought that it mouldered beneath the black veil! You see, he knew that everyone who was so concerned about his black veil was looking at it, not the man behind it. We judge by what we see, not by what is behind what we see. This was a good man, but people could not put that black veil out of their minds. You stand outside a church on Sundays and you will see people file past in piousness in their Sunday best. What have they been doing all week? Have they been practicing greed in business, have they been bearing false witness agin their neighbours? The exterior is a poor judge of the interior."

**The Real Jesus Seen in Black and White**
**From the Resurrected Spirit of Dixon Frye**

"I understand Granddaddy," I eagerly offered. "People saw him as evil because of his black veil. We all wear a veil of sorts when we hide our real selves. People who are religious on Sunday but do not practice their religion the other six days are hiding behind their own black veil, concealing their hypocrisy. They condemn others when they should be condemning themselves. They find fault with people when they should be finding fault with themselves."

"Got it boy," replied my dear Grandfather.

My Grandmother got up, walked to the door, wiping her tears, she looked over her shoulder and with a big smile said, "Black veil. Maybe you need one Dixon. That face is getting awful old to look at after all these years."

We all laughed. That was a night I carry in my heart with delight. Yes, I shall always treasure the tale of the black veil.

J. Wayne Frye

## CHAPTER 12
## MY HOUSE A HOME

*He who practices deceit shall not*
*be dwelling in my glorious house.*
*No one uttering lies shall continue*
*before mine own clear eyes.*
*Like the glaze covering an earthen vessel*
*are fervent lips with an evil heart.*
*Whoever hates disguises himself*
*with his lips and harbours deceit in his heart;*
*when he speaks graciously, believe him not,*
*for there are abominations in his heart;*
*though his hatred be covered with deception,*
*his wickedness will be exposed in the assembly.*

There are times in your life when you know there is an end coming to something. You may not know what that something is, but there is just a sense that events are configuring that will alter things, make profound changes that will forever change your life.

**The Real Jesus Seen in Black and White**
**From the Resurrected Spirit of Dixon Frye**

It was late January, and the days were damp, cold and short. Sitting on the porch was a rarity on those days, but sometimes we would wrap up and still go out and watch the traffic zoom by. I was reminding my grandfather of how my cousin Monte and I used to love to stand at the top of his yard that sloped downward toward the road and pump our arms every time a big tractor and trailer would roar by, and the driver would toot his whistle, bringing us great joy. He laughed and said, "Yep, you and Monte are great buddies. That boy is something else, he could tear up anything. He touches somethin' and that's the end of it. Never seen that boy sit down in a chair. He flops down. He's a good boy though. Yep, a good boy, and so are you Wayne."

It was not common to get a compliment from my grandfather, so I felt a surge of pride. Many years later I would wonder if part of my father's problems as an adult was because his father never complimented him. I felt anguish myself, always wanting to please a father whom I just couldn't seem to please. Still, that night was one I treasure, because I always tried to be a good boy, though I often fell short. Knowing my grandfather was pleased with me, gave me a sense of euphoria. Recognition from him was important.

I noticed he had a far-away look in his eyes as I said, "Granddaddy, how come there is so much sadness in the world. You never seem that sad."

**The Real Jesus Seen in Black and White**
**From the Resurrected Spirit of Dixon Frye**

"I get sad just like everybody else boy, but I try not to let things get me down. You know I have always had to be tough. This here world ain't easy for us poor folk. You gotta be tough to survive in a country where only the rich get special treatment."

I had a question I had always wanted to ask him, but never did. It was a question I wished I had asked, but even on this night I could not bring myself to say, "Are you proud of my daddy?" Still, I would learn later that the very night before he died he had said to my dad who was famous for his dare-devil shows, which my grandparents refused to ever see for fear they might see him get hurt, "Worth, you never cease to amaze me. You do things most men would never dream of doing. I know you want me and your mamma to see you put on one of your shows, but truth is it's just too scary to watch knowing you might get hurt."

Was he proud of my father? I think the answer is a very definitive yes, but how my dad would have loved to hear it. So, to all my readers who are fathers or will be fathers one day, do not let another sun go down without telling your children you are proud of them. No matter how old, we all long to hear words of praise from our fathers.

As usual, our conversation drifted toward religion and I said to him, "You and Grandmother are going down the country in two weeks to church. You don't really like going do you?"

## The Real Jesus Seen in Black and White
## From the Resurrected Spirit of Dixon Frye

"Don't really mind it. It's somethin' your grandmother likes to do on occasion to see family. This is one of them special Hopkins family meetins." Then, laughing, he continued, "But I sometimes get a bit scared that when I go into church that the place might cave in from God's shock."

Now, the door had been opened. "You just don't think very much of church do you granddaddy?"

"Well, like I told you plenty a times. I just don't believe in no fairy tales at my age. But what bothers me most is the finger pointin'. I just can't stand all them hypocrites thinkin' they's better than other folks. In Luke it says, 'you are those who justify yourselves before men, but God knows your hearts. For what is exalted among men is an abomination in the sight of God.' Some of these people in church you'd think they was as smooth as silk."

"Hypocrisy drives you nuts doesn't it granddaddy?"

"It does, because Jesus found it the worst of sins. Remember when they said to him, 'Teacher, this woman has been caught in the act of adultery. Now in the Law Moses commanded us to stone such women. So what do you say?' This they said to test him that they might have some charge to bring against him. Jesus bent down and wrote with his finger on the ground. And as they continued to ask him, he stood up and said to them, 'let him who is without sin among you be the first to throw a stone at her.' Now, I ain't sure Jesus ever existed, but if 'un he did, now that's a man I could certainly like."

"Why do you think there are so many hypocrites? I mean can't people see what they are?"

"Oh, they know what they are, but they walk around in they's fine clothes acting all pious on Sunday, but if 'un they hold a mortgage on a widows house, on Monday they'll put her on the street. In Jeremiah it says, 'Behold, you trust in deceptive words to no avail. Will you steal, murder, commit adultery, swear falsely, make offerings to Baal, and go after other gods that you have not known, and then come and stand before me in this house, which is called by my name, and say we are delivered only to go on with these abominations.' That's what Jesus says about them, not your granddaddy. But your granddaddy is certainly in agreement."

"So," I said, "Many people are all show but they are wearing a black veil, hiding how they really are."

"You remember that story, uh, Wayne? That is a good 'un I told you that time."

## The Real Jesus Seen in Black and White
## From the Resurrected Spirit of Dixon Frye

"One of the best."

"Remember in Luke it says, 'Now you Pharisees cleanse the outside of the cup and of the dish, but inside you are full of greed and wickedness. You fools! Did not he who made the outside make the inside also? But give as alms those things that are within, and behold, everything is clean for you. But woe to you Pharisees! For you tithe mint and rue and every herb, and neglect justice and the love of God. These you ought to have done, without neglecting the others. Woe to you Pharisees! For you love the best seat in the synagogues and greetings in the marketplaces.' So, you see, Jesus was like your old granddaddy, he could see through people."

Laughing at his comparing himself to Jesus, I said, "Funny isn't it how we are supposed to rest on Sunday to honour God, but the people who want to keep the commandment about the Sabbath have no problem going to the gas station, a restaurant or the movies on the Lord's day."

"Well Jesus said somethin' about that in Luke, too. It says in Luke that the ruler of the synagogue, upset because Jesus had healed on the Sabbath, said to the people that there are six days in which work ought to be done. Come on those days and be healed, and not on the Sabbath day. Then the Lord answered him by saying 'You hypocrites! Does not each of you on the Sabbath untie his ox or his donkey from the manger and lead it away to water it? And ought not this woman, a daughter of Abraham whom Satan bound for eighteen years, be loosed from this bond on the Sabbath day?' Jesus didn't take no prisoners. He told it like it was."

"So, you think Jesus would be disappointed in most Christians today?"

"Disappointed? He'd be so angry he'd probably tear down the churches. He'd see all them hungry people, all the people with no roof over they's head and remind them finger-pointing, strutting hypocrites what he once said, 'For I was hungry and you gave me no food, I was thirsty and you gave me no drink, I was a stranger and you did not welcome me, naked and you did not clothe me, sick and in prison and you did not visit me.' He'd lay it all out for them hypocrites without a doubt."

"So, you just don't have much use for religion do you granddaddy."

"Remember I told you what Pontius Pilot said Wayne when he saw that Jesus had done nothing wrong, except offend the leaders of the church of its time. He took water and washed his hands, saying, 'I am innocent of this man's blood; see to it yourselves.' So he had enough of them religious hypocrites hisself. He let Jesus go to the cross to satisfy hypocrites. That's it pure and simple."

## The Real Jesus Seen in Black and White
## From the Resurrected Spirit of Dixon Frye

It was cold that night as we sat on the porch, but I felt warm. There was no cold at this wonderful house that my granddaddy had built with his own hands. It was the place I treasured, the place that gave me a feeling of comfort that I have never felt in any of the fourteen homes I have owned in my lifetime.

*It takes special people to make a house a home*
*I remember such a place no matter where I roam*
*I appreciate now that which I left behind*
*It often flutters about in my mind*

*It had something special you see*
*Though there were no luxuries*
*To me it was home to a queen and king*
*Who had warmth that all have seen*

*Within those walls love was born*
*In the fields granddaddy raised corn*
*The old chairs and bead board walls*
*The place where I ran in the halls*

*In the stillness of the night death's angel come*
*An' closed the eyes of he who gave me love*
*All these years my tears have dried*
*But I now see him sanctified*

*It takes special people to make a house a home*
*Now I can sit in my palace and see the dome*
*But I know what I thought was lost is not gone*
*In my heart, grandfather makes my house a home*

J. Wayne Frye

## CHAPTER 13
## WHAT YOU DO WHEN YOU ARE HERE

*There is that one instant that crystallizes clearly*
*when you know there has been a line drawn.*
*It is not a line in the sand that will disappear*
*with the timeless shifting of the winds.*
*No, it is a definitive line carved in stone,*
*in a stone that is solid and unmovable.*
*You wish there was something you could do,*
*something to stall time, arrest it, corral it.*
*Alas, death grasps all in its dark embrace.*

My grandmother looked worried. I could see the concern etched on her face, as she said with great trepidation when I arrived for my usual Friday night sleepover, "Your granddaddy is not well. His blood pressure is too high and he must rest. Say goodnight to him Wayne, but remember not to stay with him long. He needs his rest; he is a very tired man, worn out from the burdens he has had to bear for so long."

## The Real Jesus Seen in Black and White
## From the Resurrected Spirit of Dixon Frye

I could not thoroughly understand the burdens to which my grandmother was referring at that young age, for I had never seen him bend to the howling winds of adversity, but I did know about his tumultuously difficult childhood when he had to suffer the slings and arrows hurled his way by children who were taught to be judgmental and condemning by their parents. We are all subject to the whims of parents who can either guide us toward the light of acceptance and understanding, or, for far too many of us, parents who guide us toward the darkness of prejudice and judgmental arrogance.

I entered his room quietly and stood there by the doorway staring at him as he breathed heavily. Lying there, his chest seemingly painfully rising up and down as if breathing was a monumental task, a burden for him, it struck me that none of us are able to ward off the ravages of age. To me, then, 56 was old. He was sleeping, and looking down at his winkled face I felt a surge of love, a feeling that I had never been really cognizant of how important this man was in my life. It had been my beloved grandmother who had always received the most affection from me. Her wise counsel had been my lifeline to sanity in an often tumultuous childhood. I found myself suddenly crying, because I realized just how much this man meant to me. As tears streamed down my face, he opened his eyes and said, "Stop that snivelling boy, what's the matter with you?"

## The Real Jesus Seen in Black and White
## From the Resurrected Spirit of Dixon Frye

I ran to his bedside, threw myself on him and sobbing uncontrollably kept saying, "I love you. I love you."

As I mentioned previously, he never once said he loved me, and this time was no exception, but he did embrace me, pull me close to him, and as I looked into his eyes I saw glassiness as I now realize that he was fighting back tears.

He had once told me that it is better to remain silent and be thought a fool than to open ones mouth and remove all doubt. I stopped my crying, and said no more, for I did not want to seem foolish in my sudden burst of emotion. I kissed him good night, and he said, "We'll sit on the porch in the morning and talk. It's cold, but we'll wrap up and watch the big trucks speed by."

Once again, my world of wisdom revolved around that porch swing where Dixon Frye shared his insights into life that flowed like a gentle stream through a forest of knowledge filled with towering trees that soared into the sky of hope. When you are young, you do not entertain any thoughts that all this could end in the flash of an eye. At that age, death is as remote a possibility as landing on Mars in a rocket ship. Time drags inexorably by, as each day you anticipate a time when your youth will be gone and you will not have the restraints of childhood to corral your ambitions and desires. However, this night would be different, for it would be the last time I would see my grandfather. The next weekend they were going "down the country" to visit and attend a special meeting of the Hopkins family at the church. That would be a faithful weekend that would have such a profound effect on so many lives.

My last weekend with my grandfather was not one of the happiest, because he was ill most of the weekend and struggled to find words to share with me as he was so tired. There was a weariness I had never seen before, almost a serene recognition that his time was near. He seemed to want time with me, but his tired nature kept him in bed most of the weekend. Some of his friends dropped by, and as he sat in the living room talking to them I could see respect in their eyes. Dixon Frye was a man who had touched so many lives with his kindness. How many times had I seen those looks of respect as I munched on my Buttercup Ice Cream at Clyde Steed's? There was an aura about Dixon Frye, almost as if he walked with a special light shining on him, a light of hope and confidence that you were not alone in this world if you called him friend. Many years after his death, the mere mention of his name "down the country" brought a certain quiet to the conversation, a silent respect that had not been dulled by time. His legacy of never bending before adversity, never cow-towing to those in authority, never allowing hypocrisy to rain upon him or those he loved lived on and on.

## The Real Jesus Seen in Black and White
## From the Resurrected Spirit of Dixon Frye

I know he was an agnostic, but I also know that if there is a God that would condemn him to hell, then I condemn that God. It is a God with no heart, no compassion, no kindness and no soul, because Dixon Frye understood what too few Christians do. *What good is it, my brothers, if someone says he has faith but does not have works? Can that faith save him? If a brother or sister is poorly clothed and lacking in daily food, and one of you says to them to go in peace, be warmed and filled, without giving them the things needed for the body, what good is that? So also faith by itself, if it does not have works, is dead. Show me your faith apart from your works, and I will show you my faith by my works.* Dixon Frye had little or no faith, but he had works. His works were a lasting testament to a giant of a man who cast a huge shadow over the little spot of the world he called home.

On the next Saturday night, I was at the West 49 Drive-In Theatre where my father was putting on a thrill driving show that evening. Frolicking about with friends, I had no idea of the drama that was unfolding.

My grandfather got sick while at the church, and my grandmother's cousin, Almeda Hopkins, drove him home as he lay in the back seat with his head in my grandmother's lap. He was in his prize brand new Chevrolet he had only bought a year before after having the same car for 22

## The Real Jesus Seen in Black and White
## From the Resurrected Spirit of Dixon Frye

years. He wouldn't let me eat my Buttercup Ice Cream in it for fear I might spill on the nice new seats.

As they passed the drive-in marquee which read *WORTH FRYE HELL-DRIVING AT 10:00 PM* in bold letters, coming up Ashworth Hill on West 49 Highway, my grandmother felt the life go out of him. She said not a word to Almeda, just kept cradling him in her arms. Once home, she waited until my dad's show was over before sending word he needed to come home right away. Dixon's son Lloyd and daughter Willa Mae were there when we arrived. His body had already been removed, and as I stood there watching the shocked family mourning, I could not help but reflect on all those times we had sat on that porch in the swing. It suddenly occurred to me that was now part of my life that was over for all time.

His funeral was held at that little church "down the country" where the 300 seats were all filled. People stood in the aisles and they put up loud speakers for the masses who stood outside and for as far as the eye could see, lines of cars were parked along the highway. The highway patrol was called out to conduct traffic control. Never had there been such a throng of people for a funeral in North Carolina. The minster said of him. "Look about you today at the mass of people who have come to say goodbye to Dixon Frye.

## The Real Jesus Seen in Black and White
## From the Resurrected Spirit of Dixon Frye

This is a man who touched so many lives, who proved that we are all our brothers' keepers. He was a man of honour and dignity."

I thought as I heard the minister praise him that he had probably at times condemned him for questioning the authority of the church, but I believe he was sincere in his praise. He concluded with some words that still ring in my aging brain. "Dixon Frye was a man who always asked you why things had to be a certain way. We argued theology often, and most of the time I gave up in frustration, because frankly, he knew the Bible better than I do. His interpretations of it were different than mine, but he never wavered in his dedication to mankind, his belief that we are all our brothers' keepers. The turn out here today proves that Dixon Frye was indeed his brother's keeper. Rest in peace Dixon Frye, you have earned it. Moreover, you have earned the reverence of so many people. I can only hope when my time comes I can be half as honoured as you are."

The ride back to Asheboro from Farmer was about 20 minutes, and all along the way people were standing by the roadside bowing their heads in respect. We passed one house on West 49 Highway where maybe 25 or 30 people stood in the driveway. Every one of them, even the children, respectfully bowed their heads as we drove by and I thought to myself how could such a simple man touch so many people's lives.

J. Wayne Frye                    203

## The Real Jesus Seen in Black and White
## From the Resurrected Spirit of Dixon Frye

I remember seeing cops directing traffic through downtown as his funeral cortège made its way to the cemetery. People lined the streets as if some dignitary had died. My aunt, uncle and father were all reeling from the loss of someone they worshipped and adored. My Aunt Willa Mae said, "I can't believe how many people turned out for this simple man's funeral. Look, look at the streets lined with people. Why, famous people don't get this kind of turn out for their funerals."

Oh, but she was so wrong about Dixon. In his own way, he was famous. He was famous for his unwavering devotion to justice for the downtrodden, his belief in the sanctity of every human being and that we all owed each other a hand up rather than the backhand of rebuke. Oh, and his stand on hypocrisy made him friends and enemies, but both respected him.

He had once told me about dying, "When you're dead, you're dead. That's it. No one is going to remember me when I'm dead. Oh, maybe a few friends will remember me affectionately. Being remembered isn't the most important thing, anyhow. It's what you do when you are here that's important."

J. Wayne Frye

**The Real Jesus Seen in Black and White**
**From the Resurrected Spirit of Dixon Frye**

## CHAPTER 14
## ONE OF THE RICHEST MEN

*A simple man with simple ideas,*
*That's what he thought of himself,*
*But others looked differently at him.*
*They saw a heart made of gold*
*As he did for others so bold.*

*He is remembered for so many things:*
*The words of comfort that he said,*
*The deeds of kindness so often done.*
*During the depression he fed so many,*
*Sustaining the hungry with his last penny.*

*He never saw himself as special.*
*He thought it was just natural.*
*His kindness was no Godly trait,*
*As he saw the poor worthy of respect.*
*No disdain for their plight to expect.*

*Ah, but hypocrisy he could not tolerate.*

J. Wayne Frye          205

## The Real Jesus Seen in Black and White
## From the Resurrected Spirit of Dixon Frye

*It stuck in his craw like a lance.*
*"Damn those arrogant hypocrites"*
*He shouted with clinched fist high.*
*"For this your savoir Jesus did not die."*

*Some called him a guardian angel*
*Who always bent over to lend a hand up.*
*He was admired by so many,*
*But for him, he saw nothing grand,*
*Saying "I'm just a simple man."*

*So, you who call yourself Christian,*
*And quote the Bible in great haste,*
*Quick, look at this person's life,*
*This kind and simple man*
*With no Bible arrogantly in his hand.*

We are the sum total of who we are as a result of heredity and environment. I never figured myself smart, despite four degrees, despite a doctorate at 23, despite being published at 15, despite working with the Joint Chiefs of Staff in intelligence, despite at one time being the youngest university president in the USA, despite being the only university hockey coach to have an undefeated season, despite producing a movie that became a cult classic in the 1970's, despite being called by the *Los Angeles Times* a marketing genius. **Impressed with myself – yes I was!** However, my father always put me in my place, because he was a product of Dixon Frye's wisdom that tolerated no arrogance.

## The Real Jesus Seen in Black and White
## From the Resurrected Spirit of Dixon Frye

I came home for a visit once right after I had just been appointed the youngest professor in the history of the City University of New York. Hey, was I really impressed with myself. You bet I was! However, Dixon Frye's son, Worth, knew how to put an arrogant Ph.D. in his place. He looked at me and said, "So you think it's somethin' to be the youngest professor in the history of this here school in New York City. Let me ask you somethin' Wayne. When I tried to show you how to change a carburetor in a car, did you ever figure out how to do it? No you didn't. When I tried to show you how to overhaul an engine could you ever figure out how to do it? No you couldn't. You know what? When I want them things done I can do 'um myself, and if 'un I can't do it I can find me somebody who dropped out of school in the eight grade who can do it. In my opinion son, you can't do much but stand up in front of rich asshole kids and tell 'um a bunch of bullshit. Frankly, you just one of many people me and my daddy always called goddamn educated fools."

Humbled and shamed I certainly was, and it would not be the last time that my father used common sense and straight-forward rhetoric to remind me the value of being humble. Looking back on that incident, I realize now that it made me a better person. However, I do think he could have been more tactful in his approach, but that was Worth Frye, son of Dixon, and like him, he pulled no punches and always told it like it was.

## The Real Jesus Seen in Black and White
## From the Resurrected Spirit of Dixon Frye

I have learned that an education does not make a person genuinely smart, any more than having money makes you rich. You see, Dixon Frye never had any money, but he was one of the richest men I ever knew!

**The Real Jesus Seen in Black and White
From the Resurrected Spirit of Dixon Frye**

## EPILOGUE
## WALK MATCH YOUR TALK

*Long time, long time ago,*
*Memories flash in my mind*
*Of how we sat on the porch*
*In the swing looking out*
*At cars whizzing by*
*On that old country road.*
*Days when I did not realize*
*That wisdom freely flowed.*
*Now, each day I look back*
*And marvel at what was shared.*

*You were physically gone*
*When I was but a boy of 11.*
*I never knew your value*
*Until I was an old man.*
*Yet, ever once in awhile*
*In the far recesses of my mind,*
*As real as the ending day*
*It happens so often now.*

J. Wayne Frye

## The Real Jesus Seen in Black and White
## From the Resurrected Spirit of Dixon Frye

*I can see you again.*
*Can you see me, too?*

Age is supposed to make us wiser, but I often wonder if it is working in reverse for me. However, I do notice that more people value my counsel than ever before and each time I offer advice I find myself asking what my grandfather would have suggested. Time has not dulled my perceptions of his immense wisdom. In fact, I see it clearer now than ever before. There is a crystal clear clarity that forms deep within the recesses of my mind and lights the way to a better tomorrow. Looking at myself in the mirror, I stare at an aging man who resembles Dixon more and more each passing day. I wouldn't say he was a handsome man, so the physical appearance is a bit disconcerting, but my contempt for arrogance and hypocrisy rivals his. No, it actually surpasses his.

My life is winding down now, and each day I strive to leave a legacy for those I love. Whether it is building businesses, making investments for my children or grandchildren, writing or just offering good sound advice, I work at it with diligence. Yet, I reflect on a very simple man who left his children and grandchildren no material things as he was poor. However, the legacy of love, kindness and the iron-willed determination to never bow before ignorance, arrogance and hypocrisy made his family rich beyond our wildest dreams.

## The Real Jesus Seen in Black and White
## From the Resurrected Spirit of Dixon Frye

I recall sitting in that wonderful swing with him the weekend before his death when he said, "The past is done and it is easy to see it in black and white. Success and failure is measured in black and white not colour. Feelings, regrets, the point where you knows you made a mistake is right there in black and white. A villain will always be a villain. A hypocrite will always be a hypocrite. Just ain't no two ways about it. I don't like colour in particular. I think when you photograph people in colour you just see they's clothes. But when you photograph people in black and white you see they's souls. The truth don't have no colour, no shades of grey either. It is simply black or white – the truth or a lie. When they's make a movie about Jesus today they's show him in glorious colour, but you know what? I see him in black and white. I ain't sure they's a Jesus, but if they is, from what I read in that there infernal Bible that causes so all-fired much trouble in this here world, he is simple and direct when it comes to being a hypocrite. Ain't no colour to it at all. He laid it out pure and simple when it comes to hypocrisy. It is in plain, simple black and white: **YOUR WALK SHOULD MATCH YOUR TALK.**"

THE END

www.ingramcontent.com/pod-product-compliance
Lightning Source LLC
Chambersburg PA
CBHW060921040426
42445CB00011B/732